MW01486757

Visions of Yoga

By
Gururaj Mutalik, MD

Table of Contents

Dedication

*To my late parents, Srinivas and Ramadevi, who taught me the art of yoga,
the soul of Sanskrit,*

The strength of discipline, the spark of curiosity,

The gift of imagination, and the value of hard work.

*And to my late beloved wife, Mukta, who gave me boundless inspiration to
soar, while being the*

steady ballast that grounded our lives.

*She nurtured the gift of a radiant daughter and three brilliant sons. Even
in her long battle with cognitive illness, she gave me the sacred
opportunity to care for her with devotion, a test of endurance, love, and
faith that shaped who I am.*

This book, a labor of love, carries all of you within its pages.

Foreword
by Bhushan Patwardhan

It is a matter of profound honour and personal privilege for me to write this Foreword to Visions of Yoga, a masterful and soul-stirring work by my mentor, guide, and friend, Dr. Gururaj Mutalik. Few individuals have walked so effortlessly across the worlds of science and spirituality, evidence and experience, East and West, with the quiet authority and compassionate presence that he embodies.

Dr. Mutalik's journey is extraordinary. He was the first Professor of Medicine at the renowned B.J. Medical College in Pune, a towering figure in clinical education for an entire generation of students and physicians. He went on to train in medical genetics at the prestigious Johns Hopkins University in the United States—well ahead of his time in grasping the biological foundations of health and disease. Upon returning to India, he served as the Director of Medical Education and Research (DMER) in Maharashtra, bringing innovation and integrity to public medical institutions. Later, he joined the World Health Organization (WHO) and eventually rose to serve as the Director of WHO's United Nations Office in New York, bringing global health leadership into dialogue with policy, ethics, and diplomacy.

And yet, to understand Dr. Mutalik's vision fully, one must also look deeper, to his roots. Born into a humble village family, he was shaped early by the wisdom of his father, a traditional vaidya, Sanskrit scholar, and deeply spiritual being. From this sacred inheritance, he absorbed not only the language of Ayurveda and Yoga, but the rhythm of a life lived in harmony with nature, purpose, and self-discipline. These twin streams— modern scientific rigor and ancient yogic insight, run throughout this book, and indeed, throughout Dr. Mutalik's life. Visions of Yoga is their confluence.

This book is unlike any other on Yoga I have read. It is not a textbook, nor a prescriptive manual, nor a memoir alone. It is a visionary allegory, a richly imagined inward journey, cast as a climb across seven symbolic mountains representing the eight limbs of Patanjali's Yoga. Along the way, the reader traverses not only practices and postures, but profound ethical and existential thresholds: the climb of discipline, the crossing of Pratyahara's inward river, and the subtle ascents of focused attention, meditation, and samadhi.

Each chapter is a meditation in itself. Dr. Mutalik blends the clarity of a physician, the curiosity of a scientist, the simplicity of a teacher, and the humility of a seeker. His reflections on Yamas and Niyamas are rooted in contemporary relevance—whether exploring Ahimsa as moral courage, Asteya as environmental justice, or Brahmacharya as mindful mastery of energy. He weaves together personal narrative, classical Sanskrit texts, global history, and modern challenges with seamless grace. This is not

Yoga as escapism; it is Yoga as a call to engage, to transform, to live rightly in the world.

I was deeply moved by the metaphor of the "unnavigable river", Pratyahara, as the turning point between outer disciplines and inner realization. Here lies one of the central insights of the book: that the transition from doing to being, from effort to awareness, from control to surrender, is not merely a philosophical idea, but a lived, transformative threshold. It is a message our hyper-connected, overstimulated, and crisis-ridden world urgently needs to hear.

In my own work, including the book Genome to Om—which Dr. Mutalik so graciously introduced with a beautiful Foreword, I have explored the integration of modern science with ancient wisdom. That book traced the arc from biological reductionism to meta-scientific consciousness, from the fragmented gaze of genome science to the holistic resonance of Om. In Visions of Yoga, Dr. Mutalik offers a complementary vision, he shows how that transition can be lived. If Genome to Om was the map, Visions of Yoga is the walk.

Together, these works lay the foundation for a shared aspiration: to co-create a sequel, The Om Way, that unifies our respective perspectives, scientific, spiritual, and philosophical, into a meaningful pathway for humanity. In that future work, we hope to present a global, grounded, and imaginative vision for what lies beyond the Anthropocene: a new epoch we call the Omcene, where consciousness, compassion, and collective well-being guide our systems, sciences, and societies.

But that is for tomorrow. Today, we have this remarkable offering, Visions of Yoga, from a man who has walked this path quietly for nearly a century, bridging continents, disciplines, and generations. This book is not only his legacy; it is a lamp for others to walk by.

I am grateful beyond words to Dr. Mutalik, not only for his lifelong contributions to medicine and public health, but for the personal mentorship and inspiration he has given me over the years. To now write this Foreword for his book is a privilege I will always cherish.

Dear reader, I invite you to read slowly, reflect deeply, and climb earnestly. This is not a passive reading. It is an invitation to your own ascent.

Dr. Bhushan Patwardhan, PhD, FNASc, FAMS
Former Vice Chairman University Grants Commission
National Research Professor - Ayush Interdisciplinary School of
Health Sciences Savitribai Phule Pune University Pune, India, 411007,
July 2025

Preface

Yoga: A Movement Through Time, Mind, and Spirit

Yoga is far more than a fitness regimen or a wellness trend : it is one of the oldest and most refined systems of inner development. Originating in the sacred landscape of ancient India, yoga emerged not as a standalone invention but as an inseparable thread in the broader fabric of Indian philosophical inquiry. The earliest echoes of yogic wisdom are found in the Upanishads—those luminous discourses of self-realization that speak of the Atman (Self) and Brahman (Ultimate Reality). These teachings, imbued with the spirit of transcendence and renunciation, the groundwork for a life devoted to inner clarity, restraint, and liberation.

As one of the six darshanas or systems of Indian philosophy, yoga was classically systematized alongside Sāṅkhya, Nyāya, Vaiśeṣika, Mīmāṁsā, and Vedānta. However, it found integration and refinement in the Bhagavad Gītā, where Lord Krishna delineates the yoga of knowledge (Jñāna Yoga), the yoga of action (Karma Yoga), and the yoga of devotion (Bhakti Yoga), elevating yoga to a universal spiritual discipline. In this sense, the Gītā stands as one of the earliest and most revered Yoga Śāstras.

This philosophical core was later codified with precision by Patañjali, whose Yoga *Sūtras* provided a structured eight-limbed path (Aṣṭāṅga Yoga) encompassing moral foundations (Yamas), rules of behavior (Niyamas), physical postures (Asanas), breath control (Pranayam), sensory withdrawal (Pratyahara), focused concentration (Dharana), meditation

(Dhyana), and the final state of absorption (Samadhi). From here, the yogic current flowed into diverse tributaries: Kashmir Shaivism, Tantra, and Haṭha Yoga, all of which deepened the experiential dimensions of yogic practice.

In the 19th and 20th centuries, yoga experienced a powerful revival. Swami Vivekananda, Sri Aurobindo, Paramahansa Yogananda, and Maharishi Mahesh Yogi brought Eastern spiritual knowledge to the West. Maharishi's Transcendental Meditation (TM), supported by scientific research and educational innovation through institutions like Maharishi International University (MIU), transformed meditation into a global phenomenon. In Europe it was widely practiced in the form of mindfulness. American thought leaders like Emerson and Thoreau were deeply inspired by yogic and Vedantic ideas. Later, great scientific minds such as Erwin Schrödinger and Roger Penrose saw in yoga and Vedānta a possible language to explore consciousness and the fabric of reality itself. Yoga had, by now, transcended the realm of spirituality to become a philosophical, psychological, and scientific resource.

This movement culminated in a global boom. By the early 2000s, yoga was a household word. Postural yoga gained immense popularity through forms like Rajyoga, Iyengar, Ashtanga, Vinyasa, Restorative Yoga, and many others. It expanded beyond fitness to impact healthcare, mental wellness, education, and trauma recovery. From corporate boardrooms to military rehabilitation centers, yoga became synonymous with resilience, clarity, and integrative healing.

Premier institutions like Harvard, Mayo Clinic, Johns Hopkins, and Columbia began researching yoga and incorporating it into therapeutic protocols. The ancient promise of chittavṛtti-nirodhah—stilling the fluctuations of the mind—found modern validation in neurobiology, psychology, and stress physiology. The rise of mind-body medicine owes much to yoga's influence. The development also included some groundbreaking discoveries by neurologists and neuroradiologists on neuroplasticity (both structural and functional) using functional MRI (fMRI) of the brain.

Yet, this massive success brought its paradoxes. The commercialization of yoga has given rise to a global industry worth billions. Branded yoga mats, clothing, wellness influencers, and social media aesthetics sometimes obscure yoga's ethical, meditative, and philosophical roots.

Cultural appropriation, spiritual bypassing, and dilution of lineage teachings remain ongoing concerns. Nevertheless, there is a powerful countercurrent. A movement to decolonize yoga, to make it more inclusive, accessible, and authentic, is gathering strength. Many practitioners and teachers now strive to re-integrate the full depth of yoga its ethical precepts (yamas and niyamas), its introspective practices, its spiritual orientation, and its global potential for healing.

Looking forward, yoga continues to evolve. Technological tools, AI-driven guidance, and virtual retreats are expanding access while raising new questions about authenticity and presence. Yoga therapy is becoming a mainstream discipline within mental health and chronic illness treatment.

Ecologically-minded yogis are embracing simplicity, sustainability, and ethical consumption. And the global mindfulness ecosystem born in part from yoga's inner disciplines—continues to shape education, governance, and collective well-being.

Yoga's future will depend on our collective discernment: to adapt without losing essence, to expand without forgetting origin, and to practice not merely with the body, but with the fullness of being.

A Musing on "Yogah Chitta Vritti Nirodhah"

Yoga is the stilling of the fluctuations of the mind. Not movement, but stillness. Not acquisition, but cessation. Not becoming someone, but unbecoming of all that is not truly you. The mind is a restless lake. Thoughts, memories, projections—these are its waves. The self is the sky above, constant and clear. The practice of yoga is not to fight the waves, but to let them settle. In that stillness, the lake reflects the sky.

This is not suppression, but seeing. Not escape, but arrival. In the clarity that comes, the seer abides in his own true nature. Yoga is that return. I conclude with a timeless prayer from the Brihadaranyaka Upanishad.

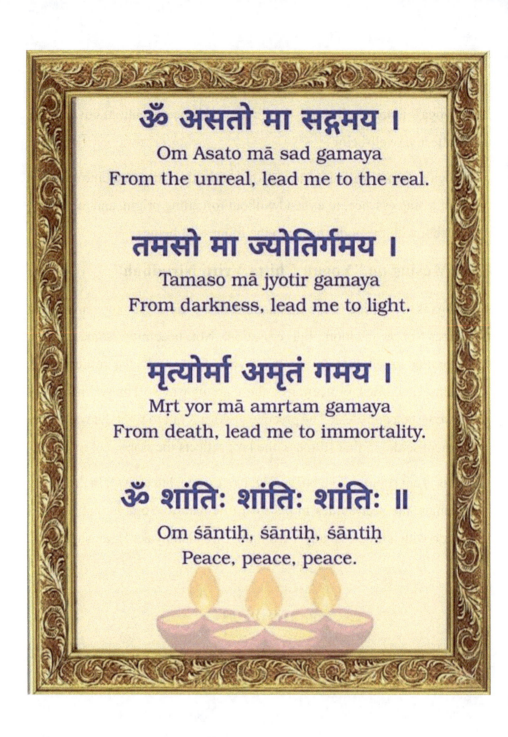

ॐ असतो मा सद्गमय ।

Om Asato mā sad gamaya
From the unreal, lead me to the real.

तमसो मा ज्योतिर्गमय ।

Tamaso mā jyotir gamaya
From darkness, lead me to light.

मृत्योर्मा अमृतं गमय ।

Mṛt yor mā amṛtam gamaya
From death, lead me to immortality.

ॐ शांतिः शांतिः शांतिः ॥

Om śāntiḥ, śāntiḥ, śāntiḥ
Peace, peace, peace.

x

Opinions about the Visions of Yoga from Distinguished Persons

1. *Visions of Yoga* is a timeless little Master Piece describing the roots of Yoga succinctly and at the same time in depth.

   It is a systematic guide to ethical and existential development, where the goal is to achieve self-insight and inner freedom. Each step is an integral part of the whole and they are woven together both in practice and in purpose in a poetic and most beautiful way.

   We embark on an inner journey of yoga through a series of allegorical reveries—drawn in part from the author´s more than 85 years of yoga and meditation practices.

   Visions of Yoga also shows how these ancient practices are applicable, step by step in our modern and turbulent life at the individual, societal and global level.

   The book is a must read for anyone interested in a wholesome view of oneself, the world and its future.

   - **Ola Schenström, MD, leading Mindfulness teacher in Sweden**
     (Former Chair of the Executive Committee of IPPNW, Nobel Peace Prize Laureate 1985)

2. *Visions of Yoga* is a profound and inspiring exploration of the timeless wisdom of yoga, presented through the vivid allegory of an inward and upward climb across seven symbolic mountains. Drawing from Your personal practice, reflection, and service, you have reframed

Patanjali's eight limbs of yoga as a spiritual journey marked by discipline, purification, and the transformative crossing of the "unnavigable river" of Pratyahara.

What makes this book unique is its ability to bridge ancient wisdom with modern life. With the clarity of a physician, the curiosity of a scientist, and the humility of a seeker, you have illuminated how yoga provides not only a spiritual path but also a practical compass for today's world—offering ethical grounding, mental resilience, and inner peace amid modern turmoil and disconnection.

The writing is humble, heartfelt, and honest. Despite your decades of immersion, you openly acknowledged that true yogic realization requires more than knowledge or practice—it demands inner purity, humility, and the gradual dissolution of ego. This sincerity makes the book accessible and deeply moving.

Visions of Yoga is not a textbook or prescriptive manual, but a meditation, a guide, and an invitation. It is a visually guided journey that takes you on a flight of commitment, discipline, dedication to inner perfection. It calls readers to engage with yoga not as escapism, but as a lived path to harmony, clarity, and purpose. A timeless work that will inspire seekers at every stage of the journey.

- Saurabh K. Chokshi, M.D. MBA, F.A.C.C.
Senior Cardiologist and Associate Clinical Professor of Medicine, University S Fla College of Medicine

3. This is a wonderful book, a great achievement. It is not just a translation of Patanjali's Ashtanga Yoga, but a unique rendering of it from the authors experience and perspective. I liked the allegorical approach and the final resolution of the story. His depth of knowledge and direct experience is pretty evident.

Love the concept of Bimba and Pratibimba. This is how I look at nature and do photography. I am fully present. I forget myself and just get merged in the natural beautiful ecosystem. I feel one with it. I love it. Nature is divine for me. We are essential participants in it…. Please let us know who did the amazing artwork. You probably have something more to say about each of the paintings.

- **Vinod D Deshmukh, MD, PhD, DSc.**
Neurologist in Jacksonville, Florida, USA. He was an Associate Professor (Emeritus) of Neurology at the University of Florida. He has published six books.

4. I was overwhelmed with joy to write about *Visions of Yoga* by Dr. Gururaj Mutalik (M.D) who was my teacher.

In Foreword to this book at the outset yoga is defined in the first sentence and is explained which creates interest in the book. To excel in life, to transcend, to be self-aware and to go beyond ordinary consciousness is achieved by Yoga is the deep meaning of the sentence.

Out of the various important hints given in this book, consultation of professionals and seeking of a proper Guru (Yoga-teacher) are the most helpful hints.

The take-home lessons and the basic preparatory steps given in the description of journey through mount of meditation (dhyanadri) are the essential inclusions. Samadhi, the ultimate bliss, is explained as merging of Atman (self) with Brahman is very well explained. I am sure that the author must have experienced it. Thus this Yogashastra has been visualised and experienced very well throughout the book. yoga beyond the mat, such as chair Yoga, is very interesting and practical part for many who aspire for yoga, but are unable to practice it in a routine way.

I will like to call him a Yogi, because of his sadhana (ascetic practice), throughout his career and gaining a siddhi of writing such scriptures. I can only express my gratitude with a thought expressed in a famous ancient quotation:

"I bow my guru who opened my eyes with a beam of knowledge, which till then were closed in the darkness of ignorance."

- Dr. Mandakini Sudhakar Pansare*
(*Dr Pansare is a professor in Physiology at B.J. Medical college and had the great distinction in obtaining a PHD in Yoga from Savitribai Phule University, India at the age of 80 years.)

Introduction

I have written this book because I believe the timeless wisdom of Yoga, often perceived as complex or esoteric, can be made accessible and deeply meaningful to everyone. My intention is to illuminate these ancient truths in a way that resonates with contemporary life, offering practical insights for navigating our world with greater clarity and purpose. It's a journey I felt compelled to share, hoping to inspire your own exploration of these timeless principles. In a time when we grapple with a multitude of existential problems – from the pervasive anxieties of modern life and the challenges to mental well-being, to the deep ecological crises and the search for connection in a digitally saturated world – the ancient wisdom of Yoga offers a vital compass. The teachings provide not just solace but tangible frameworks for understanding ourselves and our place in the universe, guiding us towards greater harmony and resilience in the face of these contemporary dilemmas.

In a world reeling from unprecedented change and pervasive disconnection, the urgent search for meaning and stability has never been more critical. The clamor of modern life often drowns out inner wisdom, leaving us adrift. Yet, ancient traditions offer guidance. Among these, Yoga stands as a timeless path to harmony, clarity, and purpose—a comprehensive map for navigating the human condition, far beyond mere material existence and its often-sleepwalking state.

This book, Visions of Yoga, invites you on an allegorical journey: an inward and upward climb. It is born from years of dedicated practice and contemplation, unveiling insights crucial for our contemporary world. For over three-quarters of a century, yoga has been a steadfast companion in my life, subtly guiding me through a bustling professional career and then intensively practiced for the past twenty-five years since retirement. This enduring engagement is deeply experiential, cultivated through continuous immersion in its tenets and diligent study of the original Patanjali's Yoga Sutras. This wisdom draws from the ancient storehouse of knowledge contained in the Upanishads and the Bhagavad Gita. Originating from the East, this wisdom has spread globally, now practiced in myriad forms and variations such as Astanga Yoga, Hatha Yoga, Raja Yoga, Transcendental Meditation, and mindfulness. My journey began under the extraordinary tutelage of my father, a true Yogi whose life embodied selfless service and wisdom. Though he had little formal education, he was a self-taught Sanskrit scholar and Ayurvedic practitioner, serving a primitive village community from 1890 to 1975. He instilled in us a rigorous yet loving discipline, fostering boundless curiosity and the lesson that "work is worship". This foundational upbringing, steeped in ancient wisdom and practical altruism, laid the groundwork for my lifelong exploration.

It is from this unique vantage point—a life bridging ancient Indian wisdom with modern scientific pursuits, from the village clinic to service with the World Health Organization—that my understanding of Yoga evolved. This continuous practice and reflection have not only granted me a stress-free life but have also yielded insights into its intricate components and overarching mechanisms. At times, these have manifested as "visions", almost like revelations, illuminating the deepest truths of this ancient science. These are the insights, born of deep study, consistent practice, and lived experience, that I feel compelled to share.

The Allegory of the Seven Mountains and the Unnavigable River

To convey the multi-layered depth and transformative power of yoga, a linear exposition often falls short. This is precisely why imagery is not merely useful, but often necessary, to grasp such an abstract and subject. Our minds are innately wired to process visual information. By grounding abstract concepts in concrete mental representations, imagery makes them more accessible and memorable. It allows us to build mental models, explore complex relationships as if they were tangible, and simulate the journey of transformation that yoga entails. Through allegories and vivid descriptions, we can bridge the gap between intellectual understanding and lived experience, making the subtle truths of yoga resonate more deeply.

Therefore, this book frames the path of yoga as an allegorical journey: an inward and upward climb across seven formidable mountains, representing the eight limbs of yoga. This journey is not without its pivotal challenges, marked by a critical threshold: the formidable, unnavigable river of Pratyahara, which dramatically separates the initial preparatory stages from the deeper meditative realms.

The first four mountains represent the preparatory limbs: **Yamas**, **Niyamas**, **Asana**, and **Pranayama**. Each mountain is a unique landscape, requiring specific efforts, cultivating distinct virtues, and offering its own vistas of understanding. These initial climbs are about purifying and strengthening the instrument—the body and mind—preparing the aspirant for the significant internal shifts to come. They demand discipline, self-observation, ethical discernment, and conscious engagement with the physical and energetic dimensions of being.

But then comes the great divide: the **River of Pratyahara**. This is not a river one can simply ford or bridge with continued external effort. Its "unnavigable" nature signifies a fundamental shift in consciousness, a radical turning inward of the senses. It represents the crucial transition from outward engagement to internal absorption. Crossing this river is less about physical prowess and more about a psychological and spiritual reorientation—letting go of external distractions to fully embrace the inner landscape. It is the moment where the preparatory limbs give way to the truly meditative ones, where the focus moves from control and preparation to deep internal experience and realization.

Beyond Pratyahara lie the three meditative mountains: **Dharana**, **Dhyana**, and **Samadhi**. These are the peaks of concentrated focus, meditation, and ultimate absorption. The ascent here demands a different kind of strength, a refined subtlety of mind, and an unwavering commitment to the inner journey. Each of these mountains represents a progressive deepening of consciousness, leading ultimately to states of unity and insight that transcend ordinary experience to enable proximity to ultimate reality.

Why This Vision Now?

My motivation to chronicle these "visions" extends beyond personal sharing; it is rooted in a serious concern, one I humbly share with many thought leaders of our era, for the present and future of humanity. We are living through an era where ethical frameworks are strained, and rapid technological advancement, coupled with social and environmental anxieties, leaves individuals feeling overwhelmed and disconnected. The very fabric of human dignity and harmonious coexistence seems threatened.

In such a critical juncture, the ancient wisdom of yoga offers not just solace but a practical, actionable path forward. It provides a blueprint for ethical living, self-care, grounding, vital energy management, and offers direction and hope to men and women of all ages, including the challenging journey into one's own consciousness for advanced seekers. This wisdom, cultivated through millennia, holds the kernel of truth necessary to preserve the spark—the inherent human capacity for goodness, clarity, and conscious evolution—for a better day to come.

I have no illusions that these vivid, though valid, insights are products of my own imagination and visual thinking. While they illuminate the theoretical path, they do not, by themselves, make me a true yogi. But without doubt, they generate a deep motivation to strive hard to embrace the wisdom of yoga and to at least work diligently toward living a yogic life for the remainder of my days. I believe that this is the way to learn and practice yoga. Like many things in life, it may seem easy to learn, but it is a hard climb.

The Katha Upanishad describes it in its clarion call for awakening:

उत्तिष्ठतजाग्रत प्राप्य वरान्निबोधत । क्षुरस्य धारा निशिता दुरत्ययादुर्गं पथस्तत्कवयो वदन्ति ॥

uttiṣṭhata jāgrata prāpya varānnibodhata | kṣurasya dhārā niśitā duratyayā durgaṃ pathastatkavayo vadanti

Arise, awake; having reached the great, learn; the edge of a razor is sharp and impassable; that path, the intelligent say, is hard to go by.

The climb is so difficult it may, as the Gita avers, take many lives of introspective meditation. But ordinary mortals need not give up, as the prize lies amazingly within the process itself. Again, as the Gita encourages, engage on this climb without hesitation—a little progress on this path is rewarded by protection from the engulfing misery and fear inherent in material life.

This work is therefore a heartfelt offering, an invitation to explore a path that has stood the test of time, revealed through the lens of a life lived in its embrace. May this allegorical climb inspire you to embark on your own inward and upward journey, to discover the deep-seated visions that lie within, and to contribute to the preservation of that vital spark for the future.

A Final Word of Caution

Many excellent books on Yoga have been written by renowned experts, and it's important to clarify my position. Despite my lifelong familiarity, studies, and practice of Yoga since childhood—and having benefited immensely from my inner journey at 96 years old—I don't claim to be a true Yogi. I am conscious that to emerge as a true Yogi, mere knowledge and long practice aren't enough. One must attain some form of Siddhi (liberated state), transforming at each stage through inner purity, eschewing every shred of ego, and rising to attain a state of total inner tranquility.

As the Bhagavad Gita beautifully states, *"Bahoonam janmamanama ante jnyan mam prapadyate,"* meaning it takes not just one lifetime but many births to attain the true enlightenment of knowledge (and its absorption) and enter the Kingdom of Bliss.

At the same time, whatever effort you make in this direction, however seemingly inadequate, always reduces the turmoil of Samsara and counters the agony of material engagement. So, with humility at heart, let us climb these mountains and cross the river together, with faith, hope, and dedication.

Mount of Inner Righteousness (Yamadri)

In the stillness of the early morning, I found myself in a tranquil state of meditation in my backyard. The first light of dawn painted the world in hues of gold and lavender, and the gentle chirping of early birds created a picturesque image of nature that lifted my spirit. Before me, my backyard pond mirrored the awakening sky. As I settled deeper into my meditation, a vision began to take form—a towering mountain materializing in my mind's eye, an enigmatic silhouette against the canvas of the dawn. This was no ordinary mountain; it was the Yamas Mountain, a vast range embodying the foundational principles of yoga. I felt a deep sense of privilege as I prepared to explore its inner secrets, understanding that this would be a visionary journey into self-discovery.

Non-Violence (Ahimsa)

The journey began with the ascent of the first, smaller hill, representing Ahimsa or Nonviolence, a part of the greater Yamas Mountain range. As I ascended, I noticed the landscape transforming around me. The air grew fragrant with the scent of blooming flowers, and the sound of rustling leaves whispered promises of wisdom. I soon arrived at a beautiful clearing, where a serene pond lay nestled in the heart of nature, its waters glistening like jewels in the morning light. Here, I found a natural stone seat, intricately carved and inviting me to pause and reflect.

As I settled onto the cool stone, the first thing that occurred to me was Patanjali's genius in defining Ahimsa. In Patanjali's Yoga Sutras, the definition of ahimsa, the first of the five Yamas (ethical guidelines), is:

अहिंसाप्रतिष्ठायांवैरत्यागः

(ahiṁsā pratiṣṭhāyām vairatyāgaḥ)

"Through the establishment of non-injury, (the state of) hostility is abandoned."

In a world overbrimmed with hostilities, this ancient insight felt remarkably pertinent, setting the stage for my understanding of this fundamental principle. In essence, the sutra suggests that when one is deeply rooted in the practice of ahimsa, there is a natural shedding of negative feelings like hostility and animosity. The presence of someone firmly grounded in ahimsa generates a space where entrenched negative emotions tend to dissolve and disappear, creating an environment of peace and harmony.

I pondered the meaning of non-violence. It became clear to me that nonviolence transcends the absence of physical harm; it is an active commitment to compassion and kindness towards all living beings. In this peaceful sanctuary, I was reminded of the power of thoughts and words, realizing that they could either uplift or inflict harm. The essence of Ahimsa called me to cultivate love and understanding not only towards others but also towards myself.

Ahimsa may superficially sound like a passive concept, but a practitioner of non-violence understands that one must go beyond merely preventing harm inflicted on others, whether wittingly or unwittingly. We must also cultivate within our being the capacity to wipe away tears, console others, and offer support to the victims of violence. It demands an active engagement with suffering, transforming passive non-harm into compassionate intervention.

This applies not only to individual interactions but also to broader societal and global contexts. Consider the numerous armed conflicts ongoing around the world, sometimes over a hundred simultaneously. True Ahimsa calls for addressing these global hostilities, recognizing that nonviolence needs to be considered not only individually but on a global scale, striving for peace and reconciliation. History offers great examples of outstanding leaders who wielded non-violence as a potent force against oppressive authority, for the betterment of communities and nations, and for righting historical wrongs. Figures like Mahatma Gandhi, Nelson Mandela, and Martin Luther King Jr. demonstrated that true power lies not in inflicting pain, but in unwavering adherence to non-violence, transforming societies through moral courage and compassionate action.

Mahatma Gandhi, through his philosophy of Satyagraha (truth-force or soul-force), led India to independence from British colonial rule. His campaigns of non-violent civil disobedience, including the Salt March and boycotts, mobilized millions and exposed the moral bankruptcy of oppression, proving that peaceful resistance could overcome brute force. Similarly, Nelson Mandela, after 27 years of incarceration for his fight against apartheid in South Africa, emerged from prison not with bitterness, but with a steadfast commitment to reconciliation and nonracial democracy.

His leadership guided South Africa through a peaceful transition, preventing a civil war and establishing a new era of equality. In the United States, Martin Luther King Jr. spearheaded the Civil Rights Movement, employing non-violent protests, boycotts, and marches to challenge segregation and discrimination. His unwavering dedication to peaceful resistance, inspired by Gandhi, led to landmark legislation like the Civil Rights Act of 1964 and the Voting Rights Act of 1965, securing significant freedoms and dignity for African Americans, the descendants of slaves. John F. Kennedy, in his Profiles in Courage, highlighted the moral strength required for leaders to make principled decisions in the face of immense pressure and opposition, implicitly underscoring the non-violent courage to stand for what is right. These leaders remind us that non-violence is not weakness, but an enduring strength that can dismantle entrenched systems of oppression and foster a world built on justice, compassion, and human dignity. It is the ultimate expression of courage, capable of transforming hearts and societies.

Truth (Satya)

With a renewed sense of purpose, I continued my ascent to the second hill of Yamas Mountain, where the principle of Satya awaited. The atmosphere shifted, charged with a vibrant energy that resonated with authenticity. I found another peaceful rest area, this time adorned with soft, green grass and a babbling brook nearby. Sitting beside the stream, I took a moment to immerse myself in the essence of Truth.

Patanjali defines Satya (truthfulness) in the Yoga Sutras as:

सत्यप्रतिष्ठायांक्रियाफलाश्रयत्वम्

(satya-pratiṣṭhāyāṁ kriyā-phalāśrayatvam)

"Upon the establishment of truthfulness, action and its fruits become subservient."

This means that when one is firmly established in truth, their words and actions become inherently effective and fruitful, aligning with the universal order. What does it mean to be truly honest? I pondered this intriguing question as the water flowed smoothly, symbolizing the clarity that Truth brings. I realized that embracing Satya requires courage to face uncomfortable realities and to express my true self without fear of judgment. I recognized the times I had hidden behind facades, avoiding the discomfort that comes with vulnerability. In this moment of solitude, I made a commitment to honor my authenticity and to speak my truth, understanding that honesty is a pathway to liberation.

It also occurred to me that the two dimensions of speaking the truth must be deeply understood. The first is the truth in society, where the ancient wisdom says:

सत्यंब्रूयात्प्रियं ब्रूयात् न ब्रूयात् *सत्यमप्रियम्।* नासत्यं चप्रियं ब्रूयात् एष धर्मः सनातनः

(satyaṁ brūyāt priyaṁ brūyāt na brūyāt satyam apriyam | nāsatyāṁ ca priyaṁ brūyāt eṣa dharmaḥ sanātanaḥ)

"Speak the truth, speak pleasingly, do not speak unpleasant truth. Do not speak untruth that is pleasing. This is the eternal dharma (righteous behavior)."

This invaluable guidance teaches us to always speak truthfully, but with care that the truth does not needlessly hurt. At the same time, it cautions against compromising the truth simply because what you want to say is unpleasant and reminds us never to flatter merely to please. This is the eternal wisdom of the ages to be practiced.

However, the application of Satya in contemporary society presents unique challenges. In many nations, the desire to uphold freedom of speech often leads to a reluctance to hold individuals accountable for every statement they make, unless it crosses a very high legal threshold. It is typically only in formal settings, like courts of law or before governing bodies, where sworn testimony is required to ensure genuine truthfulness and prevent the misuse of words. This broader societal tolerance for unverified statements, while intended to protect liberty, can inadvertently lead to the widespread dissemination of misinformation. Reflecting on this, I recognized that genuine truthfulness, as espoused by Satya, demands a personal commitment that transcends mere legal obligation, urging us to be discerning and responsible in both our words and our consumption of information.

While this is great guidance when in society, within my being, I must be uncompromisingly objective and truthful in identifying my own strengths and weaknesses in my march upwards.

This requires the practice of real introspection. Some cultures encourage a "feel good about yourself" approach, but ancient wisdom demands that to be truly good in reality, you need to get rid of negative aspects of your personality, and that requires looking at yourself in the mirror, metaphorically speaking.

The power of truthfulness, even from a young age, is beautifully illustrated in both history and myth. The well-known story of young George Washington and the cherry tree, though perhaps embellished over time, highlights the respect garnered by honesty. When confronted by his father, his simple admission, "I cannot tell a lie," Cemented his character in the annals of American history, showcasing how integrity forms the bedrock of leadership and trust.

Similarly, the mythical tale of King Harishchandra from ancient Indian texts exemplifies an unwavering commitment to truth, even in the face of immense personal sacrifice and suffering.

He endured unimaginable trials, losing his kingdom, family, and wealth, all to uphold his vow of truth. These narratives, whether historical or legendary, underscore that truth is not an abstract entity; it is a potent instrument for our inner and upward rise, whether in the material world or the spiritual. It shapes character, builds trust, and ultimately guides us toward liberation. Conversely, the pervasive nature of falsehood and misinformation is equally damaging. As the famous saying goes, "You can fool all the people some of the time, and some of the people all the time, but you cannot fool all the people all the time." While one might be perceived as glib and smart in the short term, sooner or later, a disastrous situation will arise where people discover that their word holds no truth and that they are habitual liars. That's how the great saying "honesty is the best policy" is often quoted, and in ancient wisdom, it was expressed by "Satyameva Jayate" (सत्यमेवजयते), meaning "truth alone triumphs" or "truth prevails in the end and not falsehood." As for glib untruths or even so-called white lies with good intentions, this erosion of trust, whether in personal relationships or public discourse, ultimately leads to isolation and failure, hindering both individual and collective progress.

Non-stealing (Asteya)

As I rose from the gentle embrace of the stream, I was invigorated, ready to tackle the challenges that lay ahead. I resumed my ascent up Yamas Mountain, and soon the third hill, representing Asteya or non-stealing, loomed before me. It was adorned with vibrant wildflowers in full bloom, their colors dancing in the breeze, reminding me of the beauty of life's abundance. I found a natural stone bench, its surface warm from the sun, and settled onto it, ready to reflect on the meaning of non-stealing.

The central message of Asteya is "THOU SHALT NOT STEAL." As I reflected on this term, I found myself asking many questions and answering them. Why is stealing, which in day-to-day life is so common and considered to be a petty crime—to the extent that in the justice system a first-time offender often doesn't even earn jail time—so much underlined as a moral qualifier for a yoga seeker as to be a part of the very first edict? The more I thought, the more I was convinced the ancient sages were right in emphasizing their pivotal importance, as by not respecting the right of the real owner, stealing, no matter what and irrespective of its value, is destabilizing to society and its security. It may grow and breed seeds of violence and armed robbery. It may mushroom further into thuggery by a group. More subtly, it may become an attitudinal aberration as stealing may not be confined but may manifest in grabbing other things belonging to others—lands, property, even intellectual property—and may become even more pernicious as stealing children or even women. It may masquerade as slavery or worse, as colonialism, as was prevalent until recent times, or imperialistic conquest of another free nation, and thus may breed greed and vengeance. It is far better to nip it in the bud, responsible parents in bringing up children, and teachers mentoring pupils.

I rose to resume the climb, thoroughly convinced of its vital importance. As I rounded the zigzagging footpath, I found myself at the entrance of a cave, which I entered out of curiosity.

Suddenly, an extraordinary scene confronted me. It was an exhibition of everything precious: diamonds, pearls, jewelry, and more, all in resplendent colors. On top of the cave was a sign, stark and clear. As my gaze shifted to the sidewall of the exhibit hall, I saw a flat slate board on which a message was carved: Harken, Traveler. This treasure is priceless and unguarded.

Your own conscience is its best safeguard. One who steals anything from this treasured house forfeits their opportunity to seek progress and instead returns to the misery of the world.

I was deeply moved by the effectiveness and power of invoking human conscience to cultivate righteous behavior. After enjoying the exquisite beauty and variety of this treasure, I ventured further into the cave. There are further exhibits with clear messages that stealing is not confined to money, gold, but also air, water, land, life, liberty, freedom, ideas, faith, hope, creativity, and love. I came out to pause at a pond resting place and ponder the extraordinary adventure of the cave of treasure.

Patanjali's Yoga Sutras define Asteya as:

अस्तेयप्रतिष्ठायांसर्वरत्नोपस्थानम्

(asteya-pratiṣṭhāyāṁ sarva-ratnopa-sthānam)

This translates to: "Upon the establishment of non-stealing, all jewels (treasures) present themselves."

This implies that when one is completely free from the desire to take what is not rightfully theirs, true abundance, both material and spiritual, naturally manifests. This is the key to what the Bhagavad Gita calls equanimity, an ingrained outlook by which you equate a natural, beautiful pebble as equal to a precious stone in the human material value system. The value is not the market price nor the prestige of owning the thing, but the pleasure it gives you as a piece of art.

Asteya, I realized, encompasses more than just refraining from taking what does not belong to me. It is an attitude of respect toward others and their possessions, an acknowledgment that the universe provides ample resources for everyone. In this sanctuary of flowers, I thought about the moments when I had taken more than I had given, whether in relationships or in my professional life. I recognized that true prosperity stems from generosity and gratitude, and I committed to nurturing a mindset of abundance—one that celebrates what I have rather than coveting what belongs to others. This contemplative stop on the Yamas Mountain further illuminated the path towards inner righteousness, reinforcing the idea that genuine wealth is found not in accumulation but in the spirit of sharing and contentment.

Beyond individual acts, the principle of Asteya extends to broader societal structures. Leaders and movements advocating fair distribution of resources, ethical business practices, and the protection of intellectual property embody this Yama on a grand scale. Consider figures who championed economic justice, ensuring that the fruits of labor are shared equitably and that no one is deprived of their rightful share. Their efforts to dismantle systems of exploitation and promote a sense of collective ownership reflect a deep understanding that true societal wealth lies in the well-being of all, not in the accumulation of a few. A powerful verse from the Bhāgavata Purāṇa illustrates this profound wisdom. In it, a devotee declares:

न त्वहं कामये राज्यं न स्वर्गं नापुनर्भवम् ।
कामये दुःखतप्तानां प्राणिनाम् आर्तिनाशनम् ॥

(na tvahaṁ kāmaye rājyaṁ na svargaṁ nāpunarbhavam |
kāmaye duḥkhataptānāṁ prāṇinām ārti-nāśanam)

"I do not desire a kingdom, nor heaven, nor even liberation from rebirth;
I desire only to remove the suffering of those beings who are tormented by
pain."

This response perfectly encapsulates the spirit of Asteya, demonstrating that true richness lies not in material gain but in the capacity to alleviate the burdens of others and contribute to collective well-being.

Asteya is thus a key to our comprehension of our responsibility towards our ecology and environmental integrity. It is for us to be aware that all development must be consistent with sustainability and the preservation of the environment.

Righteous Behavior (Brahmacharya)

With each step forward, I felt the weight of the previous lessons guiding me onward. As I reached the fourth hill of Yamas Mountain, embodying the principle of Brahmacharya, I sensed a palpable shift in the atmosphere. This hill radiated a regal energy, inviting deeper reflection. I settled onto a smooth stone seat, where dappled sunlight filtered through the leaves, creating a mosaic of light and shadow around me. Here, I contemplated the true essence of Brahmacharya.

Patanjali's definition of Brahmacharya is:

$$ब्रह्मचर्यप्रतिष्ठायांवीर्यलाभः$$

(brahmacarya-pratiṣṭhāyāṁ vīrya-lābhaḥ)

"Upon the establishment of Brahmacharya, vigor (virya) is gained."

This vigor refers not merely to physical strength, but to spiritual energy, vitality, and inner power that arises from disciplined control over one's senses and desires.

Often misconstrued as mere austerity or strict control over sexual desires, Brahmacharya encompasses a broader spectrum of behaviors stemming from our inability to master our sensory cravings. In this moment of quiet contemplation, I realized that practicing Brahmacharya is to cultivate a disciplined mind, one that recognizes the distractions that hinder our inner growth. It is about moderation and mindfulness, understanding that unchecked desires can cloud our judgment and divert us from our true purpose.

As I sat in reflection, the vibrant life around me served as a reminder of the balance we must strive for. Brahmacharya calls for self-restraint, not only in our desires but in all aspects of our lives. I committed to a deeper understanding of my desires, recognizing that self-discipline is not punishment but a pathway to higher consciousness and fulfillment. This realization filled me with a sense of empowerment, anchoring me to the present moment with clarity and purpose.

Throughout history, countless individuals have demonstrated the power of Brahmacharya through their unwavering dedication to a higher cause, resisting the allure of fleeting desires and distractions. Spiritual masters, dedicated scientists, and visionary artists who channeled their energy into their life's work, often forgoing personal comforts and immediate gratification, exemplify this principle. Their ability to maintain focus, discipline their minds, and direct their vital energy towards their ultimate goals showcases the immense vigor and inner power that arises from the practice of righteous behavior. Their lives serve as an inspiration, proving that true freedom comes not from indulgence but from mastery over oneself. Thus, Brahmacharya is not about deprivation, but about the wise channeling of vital energy, leading to unerring clarity, unwavering purpose, and the sustained power to achieve one's highest aspirations.

Non-covetousness (Aparigraha)

Finally, I approached the fifth and last hill of Yamas Mountain, crowned with the principle of Aparigraha, or non-covetousness. This hill felt like a culmination of all the lessons learned thus far. Here, I was surrounded by the magnificent beauty of nature, a vivid reminder of the interconnectedness of all life. As I settled on a soft patch of grass, I reflected on the essence of non-covetousness, embracing the understanding that all property ultimately belongs to nature and that true happiness comes from within.

Patanjali describes Aparigraha as:

अपरिग्रहस्थैर्येजन्मकथंतासंबोधः

(aparigraha-sthairye janma-kathamtā-sambodhaḥ)

"Upon the establishment of non-covetousness, the continuity of the chain of the past, present, and future is revealed."

This sutra suggests that when one is truly free from attachment to possessions and desires, a deeper understanding of existence, karma, and the cycle of rebirth is revealed, as the life history of the individual unfolds within this grand cosmic design.

In this serene environment, I contemplated the impact of our covetous behavior on the Earth. I mourned the imbalance we have created, where greed has led to environmental destruction and existential threats, such as climate change. I realized that by practicing Aparigraha, we can foster a sense of contentment with what we have, honoring the delicate balance of life around us.

The principle of Aparigraha has been exemplified by many who chose a path of simplicity and detachment, not out of poverty, but out of a clear understanding of true wealth. Think of ascetic and spiritual teachers throughout history who renounced material possessions to pursue higher truths, or environmentalists who advocate for sustainable living and mindful consumption. Their lives demonstrate that freedom from excessive accumulation liberates energy and attention for deeper pursuits, fostering a sense of interconnectedness with all life and an appreciation for the inherent abundance of the universe.

With each insight gained from the hills of Yamas Mountain, I felt a clear sense of accomplishment wash over me. I understood that the ancient wisdom of yoga, with its emphasis on the Yamas as foundational prerequisites, is not merely a set of rules but a guiding philosophy for living a fulfilling life. These principles are essential for anyone seeking to embark on the challenging journey of self-discovery and spiritual awakening.

As I stood at the summit, the lessons of Yamas resonated within me, a chorus of wisdom echoing through my being. I felt empowered to carry these teachings into my daily life, knowing that they would serve as a compass guiding me toward the ultimate reality. This journey was not just about reaching the top; it was about the transformative experiences along the way that have shaped my understanding of myself and the world around me. Ultimately, Aparigraha invites us to shed the burdens of material attachment, revealing a boundless inner freedom and a binding connection to the universal flow of life, where true contentment is found not in what we possess, but in who we are.

The Descent (Recall Take Home Lessons from the Climb)

As I began my descent from Yamas Mountain, the lessons learned from each hill resonated deeply within me. But beyond my personal reflections, I began to contemplate the broader implications of these teachings in our contemporary world. In a society increasingly driven by the relentless pursuit of wealth and comfort, the foundational principles of decency, compassion, and ethical consideration often fade into the background.

In our frenzied march toward material accumulation, many have lost sight of the essence of Ahimsa—non-violence. We witness acts of aggression and hostility, not only in our interactions with one another but also in the numerous armed conflicts that plague our world. This departure from compassion raises the question: How can we claim to live by the principle of nonviolence when our actions contribute to the suffering of others on both an individual and global scale?

Similarly, the principle of Satya—Truth—seems to be overshadowed by a culture that often prioritizes convenience over honesty. In an age of misinformation and superficiality, we grapple with the challenge of discerning truth from falsehood. The courage to speak the truth has become a rare commodity, as many choose to conform to societal pressures rather than embrace authenticity. This lack of transparency not only erodes trust but also stifles the potential for genuine connections.

As I reflected on Asteya—non-stealing—I recognized how modern society often embodies a mindset of entitlement, where individuals take more than what is necessary, neglecting the principle of respect for others' resources. The rampant consumerism we see today is an indication of this distortion; we have been conditioned to believe that our worth is tied to our possessions, leading to an endless cycle of accumulation that ultimately leaves us unfulfilled.

Furthermore, the exploitation of natural resources, driven by greed, has led to devastating consequences for our planet, a clear violation of Asteya on a collective scale. Brahmacharya—Righteous Behavior—calls us to cultivate self-discipline, yet the distractions of modern life often pull us away from this pursuit. In a world saturated with instant gratification, we face the challenge of restraining our desires and redirecting our energy toward meaningful growth. The noise of social media, consumer culture, and constant competition can drown out the inner voice that guides us toward moderation and mindfulness.

Lastly, as I contemplated Aparigraha—non-covetousness—I felt a sense of urgency to address the widening disparities in our world. The incessant desire for more has led to a culture of division, where individuals seek power over others instead of striving for collective harmony.

This covetous mindset not only fuels societal conflicts but also blinds us to the interconnectedness of all life. In this moment of reflection, I realized that the teachings of the Yamas are not merely ancient wisdom; they are essential guidelines for navigating the complexities of modern existence. By reconnecting with these principles at individual and collective levels, we can begin to mend the fractures in our society and foster a culture that prioritizes the greater good. The journey up Yamas Mountain was not simply a personal exploration; it was a call to action for all of us to embody these values and strive for a more compassionate and ethical world to counter the existential problems of our era.

Practical Steps Learnt During the Climb

Here are some practical steps to help you cultivate the Yamas in your daily life, especially for young people:

- **Ahimsa - Non-violence:**
  - Think before you speak: Words can hurt as much as actions. Before you say something, ask yourself if it's kind, necessary, or true.
  - Be a peacemaker: When you see friends arguing, try to help them find a solution instead of taking sides or making things worse.
  - Care for all living things: Be gentle with animals, plants, and the environment. Every living being deserves respect.
  - Practice self-compassion: Treat yourself with kindness and understanding, just as you would a good friend. Don't be overly harsh on yourself when you make mistakes, so long as you don't gloss over them or justify them through rationalization.

- **Satya - Truth:**
  - Be honest with yourself: Take time to reflect on your actions and feelings without pretending they're something they're not.
  - Speak your truth with respect: It's important to be honest, but also to consider how you say things. You can be truthful without being hurtful.
  - Check your facts: In today's world, there's a lot of information out there. Before you share something, make sure it's accurate and not just a rumor. Remember that everything you read from printed material may not be accurate.
  - Own your mistakes: If you do something wrong, admit it. It builds trust and shows integrity. Apologize if you have offended somebody, irrespective of their age.

- **Asteya - Non-stealing:**
  - Ask before you take: Always get permission before using someone else's belongings, ideas, or even their time.

  - Respect shared resources: Think about things like school supplies, library books, or public spaces. Use them responsibly so everyone can benefit.

  - Give credit where it's due: If you use someone else's idea or work in a project, make sure to acknowledge them. That's how we respect intellectual property.

  - Be mindful of the planet's resources: Don't waste water, electricity, or food. These are resources that belong to everyone, and we have a responsibility to use them wisely.

- **Brahmacharya - Righteous Behavior:**
  - Focus on your goals: When you're studying or working on a project, try to minimize distractions. This helps you concentrate and achieve your best.

  - Balance screen time with other activities: It's easy to get caught up in games or social media. Make sure you're also spending time outdoors, reading, or connecting with friends and family in person.

  - Listen to your body: Know when to rest, when to eat, and when to be active. Taking care of your physical well-being helps you think clearly.

  - Choose positive influences: Surround yourself with friends and activities that encourage you to be your best self, rather than those that pull you down.

o Be mindful in relationships: When you're in a relationship, especially after falling in love and taking steps together, it's vital to think about your partner's long-term plans and feelings. Understanding your rights and responsibilities to each other helps prevent hurt and builds a strong, respectful connection.

- **Aparigraha - Non-covetousness:**
  o Appreciate what you have: Instead of always wanting the newest gadget or toy, take time to be grateful for the things you already possess.

  o Declutter your space: Getting rid of things you don't need can make you feel lighter and freer. It shows you don't need to hold onto everything.

  o Share with others: If you have more than enough, consider sharing with those who have less. This could be toys, clothes, or even your time.

  o Find joy in experiences, not just possessions: Memories of adventures, learning new skills, or spending time with loved ones often bring more lasting happiness than material things.

  o Be cautious about endless accumulation: While it's good to be responsible with resources, be mindful of an "acquisition mentality" where you constantly strive to gather more and more assets. In many situations, one person's gain comes at another's expense (a "zero-sum game"), and true contentment isn't found in having the most.

Reconnoitering the Next Ascent

With a heart full of gratitude and anticipation, I stood at the base of Yamas Mountain, its lessons etched deeply within me. I was eager to embark on the next climb to the Niyamas—the mountain of basic rules that would further illuminate my path toward the wisdom of yoga. This journey had just begun, and I was ready to embrace all that lay ahead.

Mount of Basic Rules (Niyamadri)

Having descended the slopes of Yamas Mountain, my spirit felt lighter, imbued with a newfound ethical grounding. The journey had been transformative, revealing the interconnectedness of my actions with the well-being of the world. Now, with a heart full of anticipation, I stood at the base of the next great ascent: Niyamadri, the Mount of Basic Rules.

This mountain, though perhaps less outwardly imposing than Yamas, presented a distinct and purposeful configuration. Its decisive air and the unmade, yet remarkably orderly, pathways seemed designed to purify, to help one acquire inner power and energy.

This power, I felt, was intrinsically linked to the constant acquisition of knowledge through study, leading to the conviction that every individual is enabled and empowered by the universal consciousness, which is another name for God, existing within us. This mysterious force shapes the creation of this beautifully symmetric universe of which we are an integral part. Mount Niyamadri is constituted by five adjoining hills, each representing a core principle: **Saucha** (Purity), **Santosha** (Contentment), **Tapas** (Austerity/Discipline), **Svadhyaya** (Self-study), and **Ishvara Pranidhana** (Surrender to a Higher Power).

Purity (Saucha)

My first steps onto Niyamadri led me along a winding path that ascended gently through a grove of ancient, fragrant cedar trees. Sunlight dappled through their branches, illuminating patches of moss and wildflowers. The path felt cleaner, almost as if the very ground beneath my feet was encouraging a sense of order and tidiness. As I walked, a feeling of inner calm began to settle over me, a quiet anticipation for the first teaching of the Niyamas. I soon arrived at a serene, sun-drenched clearing, where a crystal-clear spring bubbled forth from the earth, its waters reflecting the azure sky. This was my first stop, dedicated to Saucha, or Purity.

Patanjali defines Saucha (Purity) in the Yoga Sutras as:

शौचात् स्वाङ्गजुगुप्सा परैरसंसर्गः

(śaucāt svāṅga-jugupsā parair-asaṁsargaḥ),

which translates to: "From purity arises diminishing preoccupation with bodily desires and lessening preoccupation with relationships."

At first glance, this might sound negative, but its meaning is much deeper. Patanjali is not suggesting rejection of the body or relationships. Instead, he is pointing to a higher awareness that comes through inner and outer cleanliness. When we practice Saucha, we begin to see the body as temporary and in constant need of care and balance. We no longer obsess over it or become overly identified with its appearance or desires.

Similarly, our interactions with others become less about emotional dependence and more about genuine, compassionate connection. Purity brings clarity, and with clarity comes the ability to love without clinging and to care without losing oneself.

As I began climbing, what immediately struck me was the remarkably orderly, clean, and pure environment of this first hill. It was a vivid reminder that 'cleanliness is next to godliness'. As I rounded a curve, I saw a beautiful pond formed by a small waterfall cascading down the hill, creating an amazing shower of pristine water. I witnessed a yogi completing his shower and moving in my direction. I greeted him with folded hands and said, "You must have enjoyed the shower." He smiled and explained, "Oh, it is a divine experience, cleaning not just my body but all my internal structures." Seeing my puzzled expression, he continued, "You see, for preparing yogic practice, one has to be externally as well as internally clean. That is true, Saucha."

As I settled beside the pristine spring, it's cool water inviting contemplation, I began to ponder the true essence of Saucha. It became clear that purity extends far beyond mere physical cleanliness. While external hygiene is a foundational aspect, true Saucha encompasses an internal cleansing—a purification of thought, word, and deed. It is about decluttering the mind of negative emotions, prejudices, and anxieties, and cultivating a clear, serene inner space. This spring, with its unblemished waters, served as a perfect metaphor for the clarity and freshness that Saucha brings to one's being.

My insights into Saucha revealed its dual nature: external and internal. Physically, it means maintaining clean body and surroundings, recognizing that our external environment influences our internal state. But more deeply, it calls for a rigorous purification of the mind. I humbly asked the yogi how this internal cleansing was done, and he explained that it is achieved through **Imagery**. He spoke of the ancient wisdom of the Santkumar tradition, which describes the process of internal Saucha, or **Anta Snana Vidhi** (internal cleansing), thus: "I imagine that I am standing beneath a stream of water falling from above. I close my eyes and imagine that as the stream washes my external body from head to feet, a stream also enters through my fontanelles and cleanses every organ and every fiber of my being, washing off all that is negative and unclean." It is described in the ancient texts as follows: "Tat padodakam dharam nipatanti svamūrdhani, tayā prakṣālayet svāṅgam, śālayet cāntarātmanaḥ." *"Let the stream of that sacred water fall upon one's head; with it, one should cleanse the body and also purify the inner self."* This involves consciously filtering out negative thoughts, cultivating positive affirmations, and engaging in practices that foster mental clarity, such as meditation and mindful awareness. It is a continuous process of refinement, shedding impurities that cloud our perception and hinder our spiritual growth.

The importance of Saucha is evident in various aspects of life. Historically, many spiritual traditions emphasize ritual purity and cleanliness as prerequisites for sacred practices, understanding that a clean vessel is essential for divine connection. In daily life, we see how a clean and organized workspace can foster a clearer mind and greater productivity.

Conversely, a cluttered environment often reflects, and contributes to, a cluttered mind. On a societal level, Saucha can be seen in movements for environmental cleanliness and public health, where collective efforts are made to purify shared spaces, ensuring unpolluted air and protecting the well-being of all. Moreover, the purity of intention is paramount in all human interactions; a pure heart, free from malice or hidden agendas, fosters genuine connection and trust. Thus, Saucha is not merely about being clean, but about cultivating a state of inner and outer harmony that allows for clarity, peace, and an unhindered journey towards higher consciousness.

Contentment (Santosha)

Leaving the tranquil spring of Saucha, the path on Niyamadri began to widen, leading me into a sunny meadow filled with vibrant wildflowers swaying gently in the breeze. A sense of quiet peace permeated the air, and I noticed a lightness in my step. In the center of this meadow stood a single, ancient banyan tree, its sprawling roots forming natural alcoves, inviting rest. I chose one such alcove, feeling an immediate sense of being settled, ready to explore the principle of Santosha, or Contentment.

Patanjali defines Santosha (Contentment) in the Yoga Sutras as:

संतोषादनुत्तमः सुखलाभः

(saṁtoṣād-anuttamaḥ sukha-lābhaḥ),
which translates to: "From contentment, unsurpassed
happiness is obtained."

This sutra suggests that true and ultimate happiness does not come from external achievements or possessions, but from an inner state of satisfaction and acceptance with what one has, regardless of circumstances.

As I sat beneath the ancient banyan, the wisdom of Santosha began to unfold within me. It became clear that contentment is not complacency or a lack of ambition; rather, it is a deep acceptance of the present moment and a deep appreciation for what is. It is the ability to find joy and peace irrespective of external conditions, understanding that true happiness resides within. This realization liberated me from the endless pursuit of "more," shifting my focus from external acquisition to internal richness.

My reflections on Santosha revealed its liberating power. In a world constantly pushing for more, faster, and better, Santosha offers a radical counter-narrative. It teaches us to cultivate gratitude for what we already possess, recognizing the abundance in our lives that often goes unnoticed. This practice helps to quiet the restless mind, which is perpetually seeking external validation or fleeting pleasures. When we are content, we are less susceptible to the anxieties of comparison, the sting of envy, or the disappointment of unfulfilled desires. It is a state of inner equilibrium that allows us to engage with life fully, without being driven by insatiable cravings.

Throughout history, countless sages, philosophers, and ordinary individuals have exemplified the profound peace that Santosha brings. From the simple contentment of a mendicant who finds joy in minimal possessions to the quiet satisfaction of an artist deeply immersed in their craft, these lives demonstrate that true fulfillment is not tied to material accumulation. Ancient texts, like the Bhagavad Gita, frequently emphasize the importance of performing one's duty without attachment to the fruits of action, "karmaṇy-evādhikāras te mā phaleṣu kadācana", fostering a state of inner peace regardless of outcomes.

This detachment, rooted in contentment, allows for greater freedom and effectiveness in action. Ultimately, Santosha is the key to unlocking a deep and abiding happiness that is independent of external circumstances, transforming our relationship with life from one of constant striving to one of joyful acceptance and inner peace.

Austerity (Tapas)

Continuing my ascent, the path grew steeper, winding through a rugged, rocky terrain. The air, though still crisp, now carried a sense of invigorating challenge. Sunlight beat down more directly, and I felt a subtle warmth emanating from the very stones beneath my feet. This section of Niyamadri demanded a more deliberate and focused effort, a gentle yet firm push against the inertia of comfort. I found my next contemplative spot beside a small, gurgling stream that carved its way through the rocks, a symbol of persistent effort. This was the hill of Tapas, or Austerity/Discipline.

Patanjali defines Tapas (Austerity/Discipline) in the Yoga Sutras as:

कायेन्द्रियसिद्धिरशुद्धिक्षयात्तपसः

(kāyendriya-siddhir-aśuddhi-kṣayāt tapasaḥ)

which translates to: "Through austerity, impurities are destroyed, and perfection of the body and senses is gained."

This aphorism highlights that disciplined effort, when applied consistently, purifies both the physical body and the sensory organs, leading to mastery over them and enhancing their capabilities for higher pursuits. It empowers the doer.

This Tapas, derived from a total absence of impurity or negativity—be it physical, mental, or spiritual—generates a kind of spiritual power akin to a quantum effect. By focusing intensely on something, one may subtly alter its existing state, not through external manipulation, but through the sheer force of purified intention and concentrated energy. This is the intense, almost mystical, aspect of Tapas. This notion aligns with the idea that consciousness itself can influence reality, a notion explored in quantum physics where the act of observation can affect the state of a particle. In the context of Tapas, this suggests that a deeply purified and focused mind gains an extraordinary capacity to influence not just one's own internal state, but potentially the external world, aligning it with one's highest intentions.

As I sat by the persistent stream, I reflected on Tapas. It became clear that Tapas is not about self-punishment or extreme asceticism, but rather a conscious and consistent application of discipline towards a higher goal. It involves cultivating mental fortitude, enduring discomfort for a greater purpose, and burning away impurities—both physical and mental—that hinder our progress. The steady flow of the stream, gradually shaping the rock, perfectly symbolized the transformative power of sustained effort.

My insights into Tapas revealed its role as a catalyst for inner transformation. It is the fire that refines, the consistent effort that builds resilience and strength. This discipline can manifest in various forms: adhering to a regular meditation practice, maintaining a healthy diet, dedicating oneself to challenging study, or committing to a difficult ethical stance. It is about willingly stepping outside one's comfort zone to foster growth, recognizing that true strength is forged through overcoming internal resistance. Tapas is the engine that drives progress on the spiritual path, converting raw potential into refined energy and unwavering resolve. Throughout history, countless individuals have demonstrated the awe-inspiring power of Tapas through their unwavering dedication to a higher cause, resisting the allure of fleeting desires and distractions. Spiritual masters, dedicated scientists, and visionary artists who channeled their energy into their life's work, often forgoing personal comforts and immediate gratification, exemplify this principle. Their ability to maintain focus, discipline their minds, and direct their vital energy towards their ultimate goals showcases the immense vigor and inner power that arises from the practice of righteous behavior. Their lives serve as an inspiration, proving that true freedom comes not from indulgence but from mastery over oneself. In Prometheus Unbound (1819) by Percy Bysshe Shelley, the Titan Prometheus, though persecuted by celestial powers for his defiance, never abandons his faith. Shelley captures this enduring spirit in the line: "To hope till Hope creates from its own wreck the thing it contemplates." This poetic insight perfectly mirrors the essence of Tapas: the disciplined forging of a new reality through persistent inner will, even when external circumstances seem bleak. Thus, Tapas is the transformative energy that burns away inertia and impurities, granting us the vigor and unwavering focus necessary to master ourselves and manifest our highest potential. Tapas is thus spiritual power derived from austere, disciplined living and is an important step for our ascent (Tapobala - the Power of Tapas).

Self-study (Svadhyaya)

Leaving the rugged terrain of Tapas, the path on Niyamadri softened, leading me into a quiet, shaded grove. Here, the trees were ancient and wise, their leaves rustling with what sounded like whispered knowledge. There was a sense of deep introspection in the air, a natural invitation to pause and look inward. I found a smooth, moss-covered stone, perfectly suited for quiet contemplation, and settled down to explore the principle of Svadhyaya, or Self-study.

Patanjali defines Svadhyaya (Self-study) in the Yoga Sutras as:

स्वाध्यायादिष्टदेवतासंप्रयोगः

(svādhyāyād-iṣṭa-devatā-samprayogaḥ)

which translates to: "Through self-study, connection with one's chosen deity (or higher power) is attained."

This sutra suggests that deep introspection and the study of inspiring wisdom lead to a direct connection with one's inner truth or a guiding spiritual principle.

As I sat in the hushed grove, the essence of Svadhyaya resonated deeply. It became clear that self-study is a continuous process of self-inquiry, a diligent effort to understand one's own nature, motivations, strengths, and weaknesses. It involves not only reading sacred texts or philosophical works but also observing one's thoughts, emotions, and patterns of behavior with an objective and compassionate eye. It is the journey of becoming a witness to one's own inner landscape, dismantling illusions, and uncovering the authentic self.

Svadhyaya is not just self-study; it is study for elevating, amplifying, and empowering oneself—a true means for human ascent. It demands a keen intellect, a fiercely critical objectivity, and a capacity for "reading sermons in stones and books in running brooks," adapting comprehension to a fast-changing world. This pursuit of knowledge is always geared towards seeing solutions for the greater good of the greater numbers, rooted in empathy, compassion, and equanimity.

My insights into Svadhyaya revealed it as the mirror that reflects our true selves. This practice goes beyond intellectual learning; it is an experiential knowing that arises from consistent self-reflection and the assimilation of wisdom. It means holding up our actions and thoughts against the ideals presented in scriptures or the lives of enlightened beings, not for judgment, but for growth. Svadhyaya is the light that illuminates our blind spots, allowing us to consciously evolve and align our inner being with our highest aspirations. It is a deeply personal and continuous dialogue with the self, guided by timeless wisdom. Seekers of truth across all traditions have emphasized Svadhyaya as an indispensable practice. Philosophers who dedicated their lives to understanding the human condition, spiritual aspirants who immersed themselves in scriptures, and even modern psychologists who encourage self-awareness and journaling, all echo the call for self-study. Think of Socrates' famous dictum, "Know

Thyself," or the monastic traditions where hours are dedicated to contemplation and scriptural study. The lives of thinkers like Carl Jung, who meticulously explored the human psyche, or ancient rishis who meditated on the nature of reality, exemplify the insights gained through Svadhyaya. It is through this diligent process of internal exploration and external learning that we refine our understanding of ourselves and our place in the cosmic order. Thus, Svadhyaya is the illuminating practice that reveals our inner landscape, fostering self-awareness, personal growth, and a profound connection to the universal truths that guide our spiritual evolution.

Surrender to a Higher Power (Ishvara Pranidhana)

As I continued my journey, the path gradually opened up, leading me to the highest point of Niyamadri. Here, the air was clear and expansive, offering panoramic views of the world stretching out below. The atmosphere was one of peace and a subtle sense of effortless grace. There was no specific seat, but rather a vast, open space at the summit, inviting me to simply stand and gaze at the horizon. This was the culmination of the Niyamas, the hill of Ishvara Pranidhana, or Surrender to a Higher Power.

Patanjali defines Ishvara Pranidhana (Surrender to a Higher Power) in the Yoga Sutras as:

समाधिसिद्धिरीश्वरप्रणिधानात्

(samādhi-siddhir-īśvara-praṇidhānāt)

which translates to: "From surrender to Ishvara (a Higher Power), the state of meditative absorption is attained."

This sutra indicates that surrender to a divine principle within ourselves (Antaryami) or ultimate reality is a direct and powerful means to achieve the highest states of meditative absorption and spiritual realization.

Standing at the summit, a deep sense of humility and interconnectedness washed over me. I realized that Ishvara Pranidhana is not a passive resignation, but an active and conscious surrender of one's ego and limited will to a greater, all-encompassing intelligence. It is the recognition that while we strive and exert effort, there is a benevolent force guiding the universe, and aligning ourselves with this force brings peace and liberation from the burden of individual control. It is the ultimate act of trust, letting go of the need to control every outcome and allowing a higher wisdom to guide our path.

The insights into Ishvara Pranidhana reveal it as the ultimate release, the final letting go that paradoxically empowers us most. It is the understanding that true strength lies in recognizing our place within the vast cosmic design, surrendering our anxieties and attachments to the outcome of our efforts. This surrender is not an abrogation of responsibility, but an abiding act of faith that frees us from the tyranny of the ego and its endless demands. It allows us to act with full dedication, yet without the burden of personal success or failure, knowing that our efforts are part of a larger, perfect plan. This practice fosters a deep sense of inner peace and effortless flow, aligning us with the universal rhythm.

Countless spiritual traditions and individuals of yore have affirmed the solace and power in the act of surrender. From the devotion of saints who dedicated their lives to a divine will, to the quiet faith of those who find strength in prayer during times of adversity, Ishvara Pranidhana manifests in diverse forms. Think of the concept of **Naham karta, Hari Karta in Vedanta** ("I am not the doer, but He is!"), Tawakkul in Islam (reliance on God), or the Christian notion of *"Thy will be done."* Even in secular contexts, there is a recognition of forces beyond individual control and a wisdom in letting go of what cannot be changed. The lives of spiritual leaders who guided their communities through immense challenges with unwavering faith, or individuals who found peace after surrendering to a higher purpose, exemplify the transformative power of this Niyama.

The Descent (Recall Take Home Lessons from the Climb)

As I began my descent from Niyamadri, the lessons of personal discipline and spiritual cultivation resonated deeply within me. The journey up this mountain had reinforced the understanding that inner purity, contentment, focused effort, self-inquiry, and surrender are not mere abstract concepts but vital practices that refine the individual and prepare them for deeper spiritual experiences.

In a world often consumed by external pursuits, the Niyamas offer a powerful framework for cultivating inner strength and well-being. Saucha reminds us that true cleanliness begins within, fostering clarity of mind. Santosha teaches us to find joy in the present, liberating us from endless craving. Tapas instills the discipline to persevere, burning away inertia and building resilience. Svadhyaya guides us to know ourselves deeply, connecting us to timeless wisdom.

And Ishvara Pranidhana invites us to surrender to a higher purpose, finding ultimate peace in alignment with the divine.

The notion of "God" in this context is not necessarily confined to a specific theological dogma or anthropomorphic deity. Rather, it refers to the inherent organizing principle of the universe—the All-Embracing General Organizing Device (GOD) that orchestrates the beautiful symmetry and intricate workings of creation, of which we are an integral part. It is the recognition of a benevolent, intelligent force or consciousness that underpins all existence, and to which our individual consciousness can align. This understanding transcends religious boundaries, pointing to a universal order and a higher purpose that guides the spiritual journey.

An insight, perhaps, may be useful here: We know that a vast majority of people on planet Earth believe in a God, irrespective of their diverse cultures. Science, however, often concludes that the subject of God does not lend itself to investigation by scientific inquiry based on observation and evidence. Thinkers like Stephen Hawking or Richard Dawkins, for instance, conclude that the concept of an all-powerful creator is not needed to explain most things in the universe; natural laws like gravity, relativity, and quantum sciences provide explanations. Yet, even Albert Einstein, while talking about a "clockwork universe," said there might be a "clockmaker," but his call was not to understand Him, but to know His mind. He famously stated, "I believe in Spinoza's God, who reveals himself in the orderly harmony of what exists, not in a God who concerns himself with the fates and actions of human beings." This concept of Spinoza's God, who is an enabler, a sum total of all natural laws, is far from the orthodox concept of a personal God. In my meditation, thinking of this subject, I recall a similar concept of God explained in one of the key Upanishads—The Shvetashvatara Upanishad.

In one verse, it alludes to the nature of this supreme power:

"एको देवः सर्वभूतेषुगूढः सर्वव्यापी सर्वभूतान्तरात्मा । कर्माध्यक्षः सर्वभूताधिवासःसाक्षी चेता केवलो निर्गुणश्च।।"

(Eko Devaḥ sarvabhūteṣu guḍhaḥ sarvavyāpī sarvabhūtāntarātmā | Karmādhyakṣaḥ sarvabhūtādhivāsaḥ sākṣī cetā kevalo nirguṇaśca ||)

"There is but one mysterious Organizing Power, hidden in all beings, all-pervading, the inner Self of all beings, the enabler of all actions, residing in all beings, the witness, the pure consciousness, and devoid of all qualities."

This describes a sophisticated, Spinoza-like God. By believing in God, we believe in ourselves, and by the power of faith, we often auto-hypnotize ourselves, culminating in miraculous attainments. There is power in prayers and a miracle in mantras, which have seen humanity through many existential catastrophes. God is thus not a debating subject; it is a rope thrown in our direction, enabling us to grasp it and swim through whirlpools to safety. Some do not believe in it, and we are okay with that. We do not have to hate them because they differ.

By integrating these Niyamas into daily life, we can transform our personal habits into powerful tools for spiritual evolution. They are the internal foundations upon which a truly meaningful and liberated existence can be built, preparing us for the next stages of the yogic path.

Practical Steps Learnt During the Climb

- **Saucha (Purity):** Cultivate inner and outer cleanliness for clarity and peace.
- **Santosha (Contentment):** Find joy in the present moment, independent of external circumstances.
- **Tapas (Austerity/Discipline):** Apply consistent, focused effort to burn away impurities and build inner strength.
- **Svadhyaya (Self-study):** Engage in continuous self-inquiry and the study of wisdom texts to understand your true nature.
- **Ishvara Pranidhana (Surrender to a Higher Power):** Release egoic control and align with a greater intelligence for peace and spiritual realization.

Reconnoitering the Next Ascent

With the wisdom of the Niyamas firmly integrated into my being, I looked ahead to the next phase of my journey up Yamas Mountain. The path now led towards Asanadri, the Mount of Healthy Body and Healthy Mind, where the physical postures of yoga would become the next teachers on my allegorical ascent. I felt ready to explore how the physical form could become a vehicle for spiritual growth, building upon the ethical and personal disciplines I had just cultivated.

Mount of Body Postures (Asanadri)

As I stood at the base of Asana Peak, a different kind of challenge presented itself. This wasn't about the grand moral pronouncements of Yama or the personal observances of Niyama. This mountain, I quickly learned, was about sculpting the essence of my body to conform to 'a sound body is the foundation of a sound mind paradigm.' Asanas are far more than just physical exercise. They are an effective method for building the body as a whole, not just isolated parts. Through their unique character, they intricately exercise every muscle, engaging them through intelligent stretching and a fascinating form of weight training where one group of muscles acts as the resistance for another. This brilliant internal mechanism prevents the kind of uncoordinated or imbalanced body development you see in other systems.

But the gifts of Asana Peak extend beyond mere physical conditioning. With each pose, especially as I learned to surrender into practices like the deeply restorative Shavasana at the end of a session, they provided a healthy, relaxing means of unwinding. The practice itself, with its deliberate pacing and focused attention, also created crucial periods for me to think and cogitate, allowing my mind to settle and process. Furthermore, by combining alternate breathing exercises within the postures, Asanas provided a direct stimulus for mental health, clearing my head and enhancing my focus. This peak, it seemed, was designed to integrate mind and body in a seamless dance.

Patanjali's Wisdom: The Definition of Asana

But apart from the spiritual absorption, the end of the true purpose of Yoga, its practice over long periods at all age groups undoubtedly rewards the practitioner, with significantly higher quality of life, induces a continuing zest for living, and directly promotes longevity and sustainable health and fitness. It is this dividend that explains the popularity of Yoga worldwide and its continuing rapid spread in all countries in various forms.

Patanjali, the great sage, defines Asana with elegant simplicity in his Yoga Sutras. He states:

"स्थिरसुखमासनम्"

(Sthira Sukham Asanam, Yoga Sutra 2.46).

This means: "A posture is that which is steady and comfortable."

In my understanding, this declaration means that a posture, or Asana, should be steady (Sthira) and comfortable (Sukham). It is not about rigid perfection or painful contortions but about finding a stable ease within the form. It implies a dynamic stillness, where the body is rooted and unwavering, yet the mind is relaxed and at peace. For me, this became the guiding principle for navigating Asana Peak: to seek not just the shape of the pose, but the inner experience of steadiness and comfort within it.

Encounters on the Ascent: Learning from the Yogis

As I began my climb, the path up Asana Peak unfolded into various practice platforms, each hosted by groups of Yogis. These were no mere tourists; they were seasoned practitioners—perhaps even residents of Mount Asana itself-who served as guides and teachers. Living examples of the principles they embodied, their mission was to impart Yoga Asana techniques to eager seekers.

The first platform I reached was a wide, sun-drenched terrace overlooking a cascading waterfall. Here, a group of "Rooted Yogis" held teaching sessions. Their movements were slow, deliberate, and deeply grounded. I watched one older woman, her face lined with serenity, hold Tadasana (Mountain Pose) with such unwavering stillness that she seemed to be part of the very rock she stood upon.

"Greetings, traveler," she offered, her voice calm. "On this peak, we learn to find our roots. Every pose begins from the earth up." Our teaching begins with the fundamental old wisdom:

"शरीरमाद्यं खलु धर्मसाधनम्।"

(Śarīram ādyam khalu dharma sādhanam)

— *"the body is indeed the primary instrument for the pursuit of dharma."*

I joined them, focusing on the subtle alignment, feeling the spread of my toes, the lift through my arches, the lengthening of my spine. It was a lesson in grounding, not just physically, but energetically. They taught me that true stability begins from within, a quiet strength that permeates every fiber.

Higher up, the path narrowed to a series of carved ledges, where a more dynamic group, the "Flowing Warriors," practiced. Sweat beaded on their brows as they moved through powerful sequences, transitioning seamlessly between Virabhadrasana I & II (Warrior Poses). Their movements were strong, yet fluid, like a river carving its path through stone.

"Here, we forge resilience!" a robust Yogi with a braided beard boomed, mid-lunge. "The key isn't just power, but balance between effort and surrender. Push too hard, you break. Yield too much, and you fall. Find the edge, and then breathe beyond it!"

I attempted their sequences, feeling the fire in my legs, the expansion in my chest. They taught me about conscious exertion, using my own body as a dynamic weight-training system, strengthening one muscle group by stretching another, all while maintaining an elegant flow. It was an invigorating blend of discipline and grace.

As the air grew thinner, I came upon a quiet, shaded grove where a group of "Reclined Sages" were deeply absorbed in Shavasana (Corpse Pose). Their bodies lay still, eyes closed, radiating an empowering calm. The silence was palpable, broken only by the gentle rustle of leaves. One of them, a serene man with a peaceful smile, opened his eyes as I approached.

"Welcome, pilgrim," he murmured. "After every climb, there must be rest. Shavasana is more than mere relaxation; it's a deep integration. Here, the body absorbs the lessons of the postures, and the mind finds its deepest peace. It's the moment of true healing, where the energy of the Asanas settles into every cell." Lying down with them, I felt the accumulated effort of the climb gently dissolve. It was a powerful reminder that rest is not a luxury but an essential part of the journey, allowing for physical and mental rejuvenation. They showed me that the deepest strength often comes from the deepest surrender.

Principal Asanas: Building Strength and Flexibility

These encounters clarified the essence of the principal Asanas. Asanas are body postures involving all the muscles of the body, strengthening them in a balanced manner. They are in sequence and require certain preparatory activities. They also influence the mind through relaxation postures. Each was a distinct lesson in building balance, strength, and flexibility:

- **Tadasana (Mountain Pose):**
  - **Muscles Engaged:** Engages the entire body, particularly strengthening the core, thighs, ankles, and feet. It also lengthens the spine.
  - **How to Perform:** I learned to stand tall, feet together or slightly apart, arms by my sides. The key was to feel grounded, drawing energy up through the soles of my feet, lengthening my spine as if a string pulled me from the crown of my head. My shoulders were relaxed, and my gaze steady. It felt simple, yet incredibly powerful for establishing foundational stability.

- **Virabhadrasana I & II (Warrior Poses):**
  - **Muscles Engaged:** These poses are excellent for strengthening the legs (quadriceps, hamstrings, glutes), core, and shoulders. They also open the hips and chest.
  - **How to Perform:** For Warrior I, I'd step one foot back, turning the back foot slightly out, and bend the front knee to a right angle, aligning it over the ankle. My hips squared forward, and I'd sweep my arms overhead. For Warrior II, I'd open my hips and chest to the side, extending my arms out from my shoulders, gaze over the front

hand. These poses taught me about finding power and focus even in challenging stances.

- **Adho Mukha Svanasana (Downward-Facing Dog):**
  - o **Muscles Engaged:** A full-body pose that strengthens arms, shoulders, and legs, while stretching the hamstrings, calves, and spine.
  - o **How to Perform:** From hands and knees, I'd lift my hips high, forming an inverted 'V' shape. My hands were spread wide, fingers active, and I'd press my heels towards the floor (though they didn't always reach!). This pose felt like a complete reset, lengthening my spine and invigorating my whole being.
- **Setu Bandhasana (Bridge Pose):**
  - o **Muscles Engaged:** Strengthens glutes, hamstrings, and back muscles, while stretching the chest, neck, and spine.
  - o **How to Perform:** Lying on my back with knees bent and feet flat on the floor close to my hips, I'd press into my feet and lift my hips towards the ceiling. Sometimes I'd interlace my fingers beneath my back for a deeper chest opening. This pose was wonderfully uplifting and helped counter the effects of prolonged sitting.

Advanced Asanas: Ascending to Greater Mastery

Higher on Asana Peak, where the air was crisp and the views expansive, I encountered a select group of **"Ascended Yogis"**. These practitioners had dedicated themselves to levels of mastery, embodied in poses that demanded immense strength, balance, and mental fortitude. Observing them, and with careful guidance, I began to comprehend the depth of transformation these advanced Asanas offered. They spoke of these as gateways to deeper states of awareness, requiring not just physical strength but a fearless mind and unwavering concentration.

- **Shirshasana (Headstand):**
  - **Muscles Engaged:** Strengthens core, shoulders, arms, and spine. Improves circulation to the brain.
  - **How to Perform (with guidance):** I learned to approach this posture with utmost respect. Beginning on my forearms and head, I formed a stable tripod base, then gradually lifted my legs, engaging the core to align the hips over the shoulders and extend the legs straight upward. The sensation of being inverted, balancing my entire body on the crown of the head, was both invigorating and grounding. It felt as though I had turned my world upside down, both literally and figuratively, offering a sharp shift in perspective.
  - **Significance:** Known as the "King of Asanas," it is said to calm the brain, relieve stress, and stimulate the pituitary and pineal glands. It demands complete mental focus and physical integration.

- **Sarvangasana (Shoulder stand):**
  - **Muscles Engaged:** Strengthens legs, core, and back. Tones the thyroid and parathyroid glands.
  - **How to Perform (with support):** Lying on my back, I used my hands to support my lower back as I lifted my legs and torso straight up, resting my weight on my shoulders and the back of my head. My body became a straight line, perpendicular to the floor. It felt incredibly lengthening for the spine and invigorating for the entire system.

48

- **Significance:** Called the "Queen of Asanas," it is renowned for its calming effect on the nervous system and its benefits for the thyroid, metabolism, and overall circulation. It embodies stability and inward focus.

- **Mayurasana (Peacock Pose):**
  - **Muscles Engaged:** Massively strengthens wrists, forearms, elbows, and core, and Tones abdominal organs.
  - **How to Perform (requires significant preparation):** This pose demands immense balance and arm strength. I'd kneel, place my hands on the ground with fingers pointing back, and press my elbows into my abdomen. Leaning forward, I'd lift my legs off the ground, balancing horizontally like a peacock's body. It was evidence of concentrated power and the intricate balance of the entire body.
  - **Significance:** Known for improving digestion, strengthening the arms and wrists, and increasing inner fire (agni). It embodies mastery over one's physical form.

- **Uttitha Padmasana (Lifted Lotus Pose):**
  - **Muscles Engaged:** Strengthens core, arms, and wrists. Deepens hip flexibility.
  - **How to Perform (from Padmasana):** First, I'd enter a deep lotus pose (Padmasana), crossing my legs tightly. Then, placing my hands beside my hips, I'd press down to lift my entire body, including my crossed legs, off the ground. It requires extreme flexibility in the hips and strong foundational strength in the arms and core to float above the earth.
  - **Significance:** This pose symbolizes lightness, detachment, and the ability to rise above earthly concerns. It deeply tones the abdomen and strengthens the upper body, demonstrating immense control.

These advanced poses, I understood, were not destinations to be rushed, but practices to be approached with reverence, patience, and a deep understanding of one's own body and its readiness. They were the ultimate expression of "Sthira Sukham Asanam" at its most demanding and transformative.

Adapting Asanas: Yoga on a Chair for Health Conditions

One of the most valuable lessons I learned on Asana Peak was the adaptability of the practice. For those with backache, mobility issues, or other health conditions, many of these powerful Asanas can be performed while sitting on a chair. This opened up the practice to everyone, reinforcing that the essence of Asana is not the rigid form, but the steady and comfortable experience.

For example:

- **Seated Cat-Cow:** Sitting tall, I'd round my back on an exhale (like a cat stretching) and arch my back on an inhale, lifting my chest (like a cow). This gently mobilized the spine.
- **Seated Twists:** While seated, I could gently twist my torso, using the back of the chair for support, to improve spinal flexibility and aid digestion.
- **Seated Forward Fold:** Perched on the edge of the chair, I could slowly fold forward, letting my head hang heavy, to release tension in the back and neck.

- **Seated Leg Lifts/Extensions:** To strengthen my legs, I could extend one leg straight out, holding it for a moment, or lift one knee towards my chest.

These modifications proved that the spirit of Asana—the cultivation of stability and ease—is accessible to all, regardless of physical limitations.

The Master Exercise: Surya Namaskar (Sun Salutations)

Finally, I encountered what I came to call the Master Exercise of Asana Peak: Surya Namaskar, or the Sun Salutations. This isn't a single pose, but a combination of multiple asanas linked together in a dynamic, flowing sequence. It's a devotional practice that combines movement with breath, often performed at sunrise.

A typical Surya Namaskar sequence involves a series of 12 postures, flowing seamlessly from one to the next, often including:

1. **Pranamasana (Prayer Pose):** Standing at the front of the mat, hands at heart center.
2. **Hasta Uttanasana (Raised Arms Pose):** Inhaling, sweeping arms up and slightly bend back..
3. **Hasta Padasana (Hand to Foot Pose):** Exhaling, fold forward.
4. **Ashwa Sanchalanasana (Equestrian Pose):** Inhaling, stepping one foot back, dropping the knee, looking up.
5. **Chaturanga Dandasana (Four-Limbed Staff Pose) or Plank:** Exhaling, stepping back to plank and lowering down.
6. **Urdhva Mukha Svanasana (Upward-Facing Dog):** Inhaling, lifting the chest and thighs off the floor.

7. **Adho Mukha Svanasana (Downward-Facing Dog):** Exhaling, lift hips back into Downward Dog.

8. **Ashwa Sanchalanasana (Equestrian Pose):** Inhaling, stepping the back foot forward.

9. **Hasta Padasana (Hand to Foot Pose):** Exhaling, stepping the other foot forward, folding.

10. **Hasta Uttanasana (Raised Arms Pose):** Inhaling, sweeping arms up and back.

11. **Pranamasana (Prayer Pose):** Exhaling, hands to heart center.

This sequence is a complete practice in itself, warming the body, stretching and strengthening nearly every major muscle group, and synchronizing breath with movement in a meditative rhythm. It felt like a miniature journey through the entire Asana Peak, preparing me for the next stages of my allegorical climb.

Descending with Wisdom: Lessons Learned from Asana Peak

My journey up Asana Peak and the conversations with the Yogis I met left me with deep insights. These are the takeaway lessons I carry with me, not just for my physical practice, but for my life:

- **The Body is a Sacred Temple:** Asanas taught me that the physical form is not separate from the spiritual journey. It is the vehicle, the very instrument through which we experience life and pursue higher truths. To respect and care for it through mindful efforts, physical and spiritual, is an act of reverence.

- **Listen to Your Inner Guide:** The most valuable instruction I received was not from a teacher, but from my own body. The principle of "Sthira Sukham" became a constant internal dialogue. My body constantly communicated its limits and its potential. Learning to listen to these subtle signals was paramount.

- **Consistency Over Intensity:** I realized that brief, regular practice yields far greater results than infrequent, overly ambitious sessions. The mountain doesn't reveal its secrets in a single strenuous climb, but through consistent, dedicated ascents.

- **Breath is the Anchor:** The breath is the thread that connects mind and body. It's the key to deepening a pose, calming the nervous system, and staying present. Without conscious breathing, Asana is just gymnastics.

- **Growth is Gradual, Not Forceful:** True progress on Asana Peak was never about forcing my body into shapes it wasn't ready for. It was about gentle persistence, patience, and celebrating small improvements. Each slight increase in flexibility or strength was a quiet triumph.

- **Yoga is for Every Body:** The chair yoga practitioners showed me that the essence of Yoga transcends physical form or ability. It is about intention, presence, and finding "Sthira Sukham" within one's own unique circumstances.

Helpful Hints for Beginners and Those with Conditions

For those just beginning their climb of Asana Peak, or for those navigating specific physical conditions like arthritis or backache, I offer these hard-won hints to ensure a safe, fulfilling, and injury-free journey:

1. **Consult a Professional:** Always, always, consult a qualified physical therapist before starting any new exercise regimen, especially if you have existing health conditions like arthritis, severe back pain, or other chronic issues. They can advise on what movements are safe and beneficial for your specific body.

2. **Find a Qualified Yoga Teacher:** Seek out a yoga instructor who is experienced and knowledgeable, particularly one who understands anatomy and can offer modifications. A good teacher will emphasize safety and individual needs over forcing students into advanced poses.

3. **"No Pain, No Gain" is NOT for Yoga:** This is perhaps the most crucial lesson on Asana Peak. Never push into pain. Discomfort is part of stretching and building strength, but sharp or increasing pain is a clear signal to ease off, adjust, or stop. Your body is communicating; listen intently.

4. **Embrace Modifications:** Don't view modifications (like using props, a chair, or adjusting the depth of a pose) as a sign of weakness. They are signs of intelligence and self-awareness. For arthritis, focus on a gentle, pain-free range of motion. For backache, prioritize movements that lengthen and strengthen the spine gently, avoiding poses that compress or twist the lower back excessively. Chair yoga is your ally!

5. **Focus on Breath (Pranayama's Partner):** Let your breath guide your movement. If your breath becomes strained or shallow, you are pushing too hard. Deep, even breathing indicates that you are working within your capacity.

6. **Warm Up Gently:** Just as a mountain climber prepares for an ascent, warm up your body before deep stretches. Gentle movements, like seated cat-cow or slow twists, can prepare your muscles and joints.

7. **Hold Poses Mindfully:** While some styles flow quickly, mindful holding allows muscles to lengthen and strengthen. However, if holding a pose causes discomfort, ease out of it.

8. **Props are Your Friends:** Yoga blocks, straps, blankets, and bolsters are not crutches; they are tools that allow you to find "Sthira Sukham" in poses you might not otherwise access safely. Use them liberally, especially for conditions like arthritis to support joints, or for backache to provide gentle cushioning and alignment.

9. **Consistency is Key:** Short, regular practices are more beneficial than sporadic, intense ones. Even 10-15 minutes daily can build strength, flexibility, and mental calm.

10. **The Importance of Shavasana:** Never skip the final relaxation pose (Savasana). It is where the body integrates physical work and the mind settles, preventing overstimulation and promoting deep relaxation.

Asanas vs. Gym Workouts: A Comparative Look

As I considered the diverse paths to physical fitness, I couldn't help but compare the journey up Asana Peak to the vigorous routines one might undertake in a modern gym. Both offer significant benefits, but their philosophies and ultimate outcomes differ considerably.

The gym workout, with its focus on weights, machines, and high-intensity cardio, excels at rapid muscle growth, targeted muscle isolation, and quick calorie burning. It's effective for building bulk, achieving specific aesthetic goals, and pushing physical limits. The energy is often high-octane, driven by external motivation and measurable metrics. However, I often observed that gym workouts, when pursued exclusively, could sometimes lead to imbalanced muscle development, joint strain from heavy lifting without proper form, and a tendency to overlook flexibility and mental integration. There's also the constant need for equipment and a dedicated facility.

Asanas, on the other hand, offer a holistic approach, integrating mind, body, and breath. While they may not produce immediate bulk, they cultivate functional strength, endurance, and deep flexibility, often engaging smaller, stabilizing muscles that gym routines might miss. The emphasis on body weight as resistance naturally promotes a balanced physique. Beyond the physical, Asanas prioritize mindfulness, stress reduction, improved posture, and enhanced body awareness. The risk of injury is generally lower when practiced mindfully, and the practice is highly adaptable, requiring minimal equipment and able to be done almost anywhere. However, for those seeking extreme muscle hypertrophy or rapid weight loss, Asanas alone might take a longer, more subtle path. Ultimately, both paths have their merits, and some find great benefit in combining aspects of both, using Asanas to complement gym training by improving flexibility and preventing injury.

Beyond individual well-being, I also came to realize that Asanas possess immense, untapped potential, particularly within competitive sports. With further research and experimental approaches, these ancient practices could be more fully integrated into the training regimes of athletes across all disciplines. Their inherent focus on flexibility, balance, core strength, and nuanced body awareness is precisely what is needed to minimize and prevent common sports injuries, which often arise from muscular imbalances, limited range of motion, and overtraining. Moreover, the emphasis on mindful breathing and relaxation could significantly combat athlete burnout, a pervasive challenge in demanding sports. By fostering mental resilience and aiding efficient recovery, Asanas could play a crucial role in extending and increasing the active lifespan of athletes, allowing them to perform at their peak for longer and with greater overall well-being. This vision of incorporating Asanas as a fundamental pillar of athletic preparation excites me greatly.

Perhaps the science of sports medicine, which currently focuses on the prevention, management, and restoration of vital functions for elite athletes across all games and sports, will absorb the far-reaching advantages of incorporating yoga into fitness regimes. This would not only sustain balance and strength and prevent injuries, but also promote mental equilibrium, effectively eliminating the 'nerves' that can hinder certain athletes, and ultimately lead to a significantly enhanced athletic longevity of future champions.

Conclusion: The Enduring Value of Asana

My journey on Asana Peak revealed that true strength isn't about physical prowess alone, but about the relationship we cultivate with our own physical and energetic self. It's about finding that sweet spot of effort and ease, listening to the subtle language of the body, and respecting its wisdom. With this newfound steadiness and comfort forged in the crucible of Asana, I feel better prepared to face the next challenges on the mountain of Yoga.

As I look back from the summit of Asana Peak, it is clear to me that this disciplined yet gentle approach to physical well-being deserves wider practice and recognition. In a world that often values external results and intense stress, Asanas offer a path to sustainable health, inner calm, and a connection between body and mind. They are not just exercises; they are a means to cultivate resilience, peace, and self-awareness that transcends the yoga mat and enriches every aspect of life. This fitness regime is a timeless gift, accessible to all, and its holistic benefits make it an invaluable pursuit for anyone seeking a deeper, more integrated approach to living.

Mudras: The Contemplation Platform

Having journeyed down from the vibrant, active slopes of **Asanadri**, the mountain of postures, I find myself on a serene, small **platform of contemplation**. This isn't a place for grand movements or strenuous exertion, but rather a quiet eddy in the flow of our ascent, a space for subtle refinement and inner focus. The air here feels different, still, yet charged with quiet energy, a gentle hum that speaks of a deeper connection between the physical and the unseen.

This platform, suspended between the recent triumphs of bodily mastery and the impending climb into the realm of breath, is where we prepare to harness and direct the very essence of our being. It is here that we discover Mudras, the gestures and seals that guide our internal energy, shaping both mind and spirit for the journey ahead. Hereon this platform, as I began my contemplation, my eyes closed, and I drifted into a reverie. I saw a book with a golden aura, and an unseen presence read aloud in a mellow voice, like an audiobook. This is what I heard: The concept of **Mudra** transcends simple physical form. While many are hand positions, a Mudra is essentially a "seal" or "gesture" that directs the flow of prana, our vital life force energy. Our larger body movements in Asana cultivate and distribute this energy, but Mudras offer a more refined control, acting like subtle switches that guide this inherent power. Think of our hands, rich in nerve endings and energy points, as intricate control panels; by consciously bringing specific fingers and palms into contact, we create energetic circuits. This intentional sealing prevents the dispersion of prana, turning our focus inward and subtly but powerfully influencing our consciousness, preparing the mind for the deeper states of concentration required as we ascend the coming mountains.

Beyond these more familiar hand gestures, it's worth noting that the term "Mudra" encompasses a broader spectrum of symbolic expressions within various yogic and spiritual traditions. To outsiders, certain ancestral yoga sects might engage in practices like **Mudra Dharan**, or "wearing holy symbols". This form of purification or sacred marking, distinct from internal hand gestures, still serves as a symbolic seal. Sandalwood paste is often applied to specific points on the body, such as the temples, chest, abdomen, and forehead. Sometimes, divine symbols like the **chakra**, **shankha**, or **padma** are also stamped. In more historical or deeply traditional contexts, some dedicated followers might even undergo a ritual where heated metallic patterns of these sacred symbols are temporarily branded onto the skin, by a Guru (Swami) signifying a deep sectarian or devotional relationship and acting as a constant reminder of their spiritual path, aligning with principles of Saucha (purity) in a broader, external sense.

To begin our subtle practice on this contemplation platform, we now focus on a few key hand Mudras that are both foundational and impactful. Find a comfortable, seated posture—perhaps one you perfected on Asana Mountain—ensuring your spine is erect and relaxed. Close your eyes gently or soften your gaze. **Jnana Mudra** (Mudra of Wisdom) and Chin Mudra (Mudra of Consciousness) are perhaps the most common and potent: simply bring the tip of your index finger to touch the tip of your thumb, with the other three fingers extended. In **Chin Mudra**, the index finger bends to touch the base of the thumb. Both are typically formed with palms downwards on the knees, symbolically uniting individual and universal consciousness, fostering wisdom and mental clarity. For balancing the breath, **Vishnu Mudra** (Mudra of Balance) is essential: fold your index and middle fingers to your palm, leaving your thumb, ring finger, and little finger extended to regulate breath during practices like alternate nostril breathing. Finally, **Anjali Mudra** (Reverence Mudra), where palms are pressed together in front of the heart center, instantly centers the mind, symbolizing respect, humility, and the unification of dualities within oneself.

For many dedicated practitioners, Mudras are not merely occasional gestures but an integral part of their lifelong routine, woven seamlessly into their daily practice. They act as **further catalysts**, subtly enhancing the benefits of both asana routines and pranayama. Over the years, the conscious formation of a Mudra becomes almost second nature, transforming from a deliberate act into an intuitive expression of the practitioner's inner state. This continuous engagement deepens the connection between body, breath, and mind, allowing the yogi to refine their energetic awareness and direct their focus with increasing precision. In this way, Mudras transcend simple techniques; they become a living, breathing aspect of one's ongoing yogic journey, enriching every step on the path.

Ultimately, these subtle gestures are invaluable **adjuncts** that any dedicated yoga practitioner should endeavor to inculcate into their life. They are simple to learn, yet effective tools for self- regulation and energetic refinement. By consciously incorporating Mudras, whether during formal practice or quiet moments of reflection, one can deepen one's connection to the subtle body, enhance one's meditation and breathwork, and cultivate a heightened state of awareness. They serve as constant reminders of the interplay between the gross and subtle aspects of our being, offering a pathway to bring the principles of yoga into every moment of living, thus preparing us more fully for the mysterious journey that lies ahead.

From a scientific vantage point, the burgeoning field of research on Mudras holds exciting promise, aligning with the ancient insights of Yogis and Rishis. While historical and sectarian traditions have long employed Mudras as external marks of purity and devotion—practices like Mudra Dharan—modern inquiry focuses on their internal, physiological impacts. Future studies are poised to delve deeper into the precise mechanisms at play, particularly in identifying how the stimulation of the rich network of

nerve endings in the hands might **trigger the beneficial release of neurotransmitters** such as serotonin and dopamine, influencing mood, focus, and overall well-being.

Furthermore, itis intriguing to consider how the consistent practice of Mudras, through their calming influence on the nervous system and promotion of internal balance, could contribute to broader **restorative processes** within the body. This could extend to promoting cellular health, reducing inflammation, and even activating various **epigenomic factors**. The study of epigenetics—how lifestyle and environment can influence gene expression without altering the underlying DNA—offers an avenue for understanding how these subtle practices might lead to heritable, beneficial changes, shaping not just individual health but potentially future generations.

This "Contemplation Platform" of Mudras, therefore, marks a pivotal moment in our allegorical ascent. The stillness, focus, and directed energy cultivated here are essential tools for navigating the higher climbs of breath control on **Pranayama Mountain**, where prana is consciously expanded and refined.

As my contemplation on this tranquil platform ended, a clarity settled within me. I opened my eyes, awakening from this deep reverie, having absorbed the subtle wisdom of the Mudras and integrated all that I had learned as relevant for this journey so far. With a renewed sense of purpose and a spirit filled with gratifying cheerfulness and joy, I rose, ready to resume our grand adventure and begin the invigorating ascent of the vital **Pranayama Mountain**.

Mount of Breath and Energy (Pranadri)

As I continued my ascent on the majestic Mountain of Yoga, having traversed the foundational foothills of Yama and Niyama, and successfully scaled the Mount of Asanas, I found myself gazing up at the next imposing, yet inviting, peak: the **Prana Mountain**. Its very essence seemed to hum with an unseen energy, a vibrant current that pulsed through the air, rustling the leaves of ancient trees, and whispering through the crevasses of the rock. This was the domain of **Pranayama**, the vital science of breath control, and I knew that to deepen my understanding, in the next stage of my spiritual journey, I must learn to consciously harness this life-giving force.

This mountain, I quickly learned, was about far more than just breathing air. It was about sculpting the subtle energy of my being, ensuring a smooth and potent flow of Prana throughout my entire system. Pranayama, I discovered, is a method for refining the life force, influencing not just physical health but mental clarity and spiritual awakening. Through its unique character, it intricately purifies energetic channels, engages the mind through focused attention, and offers a fascinating interplay of energetic currents, where one Vayu (energy current) balances and influences another. This brilliant internal mechanic prevents the kind of chaotic or imbalanced energetic flow you often see in modern, unconscious living.

But the gifts of Prana Mountain extend beyond mere energetic conditioning. With each regulated breath, especially as I learned to surrender into practices that prolonged breath retention, they provided a healthy, rejuvenating means of calming the nervous system. The practice itself, with its deliberate pacing and focused attention, also created crucial periods for me to process and observe my inner landscape, allowing my mind to settle and purify. Furthermore, by consciously directing the breath, Pranayama provided a direct stimulus for mental health, clearing my head and enhancing my focus. This peak, it seemed, was designed to integrate mind and energy in a seamless engagement.

Patanjali's Wisdom: The Definition of Pranayama

Patanjali, the great sage, in his Yoga Sutras, defines Pranayama with elegant simplicity. He states:

तस्मिन्सति श्वासप्रश्वासयोर्गतिविच्छेदः प्राणायामः ॥४९॥

tasminsati śvāsapraśvāsayorgativicchedaḥ prāṇāyāmaḥ

Meaning "That [āsana] having been perfected, Prāṇāyāma is the cessation of the movements of inhalation and exhalation." (Yoga Sutra 2.49)

This is an insightful interpretation of Pranayama, especially your connection to "Prana Mountain" and the emphasis on the "pause". Let's refine it to enhance clarity and flow, ensuring your understanding shines through.

In my understanding, this declaration means that Pranayama is far more than mere breathing; it is the intentional suspension and regulation of breath, allowing us to directly work with the subtle life force itself. It's about becoming the conscious orchestrator of our inner rhythm, extending beyond the simple acts of inhaling and exhaling to actively influence the very flow of Prana. For me, this became the guiding principle for navigating Prana Mountain: to seek not just the rhythm of breath, but the inner experience of vital energy flowing steadily and comfortably. Patanjali's definition aptly restores balance to our understanding of Pranayama, emphasizing that it's not merely about breathing in and out, but crucially, about the importance of paying attention to the "pause" between the two— the suspension or holding of the breath.

Encounters on the Ascent: Learning from the Yogis

As I began my climb, the path up Prana Mountain unfolded into various practice platforms, each hosted again by different groups of Resident Yogis. They have been seasoned practitioners, living examples of the principles they embodied, each specializing in a unique aspect of breath mastery. The first platform I reached was a wide, sun-bathed terrace overlooking a cascading waterfall.

Here, a group of "Rhythmic Breathers" practiced. Their movements were subtle, almost imperceptible, their faces serene as they engaged in gentle, elongated breaths. They exhibited an aura of spiritual power. I watched one older woman, her face lined with serenity, guide the flow of breath with such unwavering stillness that she seemed to be part of the very air she breathed.

"Greetings, traveler," she offered, her voice calm. "On this peak, we learn to find our rhythm. Every practice begins by balancing the streams of energy within." I joined them, focusing on the subtle alignment of my breath, feeling the gentle expansion of inhalation (Puraka), the stillness of retention (Kumbhaka), and the complete release of exhalation (Rechaka). It was a lesson in internal balance, not just physically, but energetically. They taught me that true vitality begins from within, a quiet flow that permeates every fiber, controlled by the harmonious interplay of the five **Vayus**:

- **Prana Vayu:** The invard-moving life-giver, governing reception.
- **Apana Vayu:** The downward-moving energy of elimination.

- **Samana Vayu:** The balancing force, integrating Prana and Apana in the core.
- **Udana Vayu:** The upward energy for speech and spiritual growth.
- **Vyana Vayu:** The pervasive energy for circulation and coordination.

Higher up, the path narrowed to a series of carved ledges, where a more dynamic group, the "Energetic Purifiers," practiced. Sweat beaded on their brows as they moved through powerful, rapid breathing sequences, exhaling with force like bellows stoking a fire. "Here, we forge clarity!" a robust Yogi with a braided beard boomed, mid-exhalation. "The key isn't just power, but purification. Push out the stagnation, clear the channels, and then breathe freely!"

I attempted their sequences, feeling the internal heat, the invigorating rush of energy. They taught me about conscious cleansing, using my own breath as a dynamic tool to clear blockages in the **nadis**[1], the subtle energy channels. This was a vital step, understanding that a clear network of nadis allows prana to flow unimpeded, fostering health and mental acuity. As the air grew thinner, I came upon a quiet, shaded grove where a group of "Harmonic Sages" were deeply absorbed in humming breaths. Their bodies vibrated gently, eyes closed, radiating a calm. The silence was palpable, broken only by the gentle hum of their practice. One of them, a serene man with a peaceful smile, opened his eyes as I approached. "Welcome,

---

[1] The Sanskrit word Nadi (नाडी) has a dual meaning. While it primarily refers to a tube, vessel, channel, nerve, or vein (in the context of the energetic body), it is also the Sanskrit term for river or stream. This linguistic parallelism beautifully illustrates the flowing nature of Prana through these energetic pathways, akin to how rivers carry life-sustaining water throughout the land.

pilgrim," he murmured. "After every surge, there must be balance. Here, we harmonize the opposing currents. This is where the true understanding of the nadis unfolds, revealing nature's power in asymmetry."

Lying down with them, I felt the soothing vibrations and a deep sense of peace. They showed me that the deepest harmony often comes from balancing seemingly opposite forces, embodying the wisdom of the ancient verse about Ida, Pingala, and Sushumna. An ancient verse describes the three vital energy channels within the subtle body:

इडा भागीरथी प्रोक्ता, पिङ्गला यमुना स्मृता।
तयोर्मध्ये गता नाडी सुषुम्नाख्या सरस्वति॥

(Idā Bhāgīrathī proktā, Piṅgalā Yamunā smṛtā, Tayor madhye gatā nāḍī Suṣumnākhyā Sarasvatī)

To the left flows Ida, known as Bhagirathi or Ganga. To the right flows Pingala, called Yamuna. Between them runs the hidden and all-important channel Saraswati, known as Sushumna. What a beautiful way of illustrating a symbol of their land's vital rivers, which then supported all life between them and thus sustained, as breath does, the Harappa civilization of the founding Aryans.

This taught me about the asymmetrical yet complementary nature of these subtle channels – Ida (lunar, feminine, left nostril), Pingala (solar, masculine, right nostril), and the central, unifying Sushumna. This understanding was pivotal, demonstrating that just as in the universe, true strength and creativity often arise from the dynamic interplay of distinct, yet interdependent forces.

Principal Pranayama Techniques: Cultivating Energy and Calm

These encounters clarified the essence of the principal Pranayama techniques. Each was a distinct lesson in building energetic balance, purifying the channels, and calming the mind:

- **Ujjayi Breath (Victorious Breath):**
    - o **Purpose:** Calming, balancing prana, increasing **ojas** (vitality), promoting relaxation.
    - o **How to Perform:** I learned to breathe through my nose, constricting the back of my throat slightly on both inhale and exhale, creating a soft, ocean-like sound. It felt simple, yet incredibly powerful for establishing a steady, internal rhythm and focus.

Nadi Shodhana (Alternate Nostril Breathing):

- o **Purpose:** Balancing Ida and Pingala nadis, harmonizing prana, promoting mental clarity and emotional equilibrium.
- o **How to Perform:** Using my right hand, I would first close my right nostril with my thumb and gently exhale through the left. Then, keeping the right nostril closed, I inhaled through the right, switched to close the left with my ring finger, and exhaled through the right. Inhaling once more through the right and exhaling through the left completed one round.

This practice revealed to me the subtle dance of energy within. This technique taught me about the subtle dance of energy within.

- **Bhastrika (Bellows Breath):**
  - o **Purpose:** Energizing, stimulating prana, clearing Kapha (congestion), invigorating the body and mind.
  - o **How to Perform:** I'd practice rapid, forceful exhalations and equally forceful inhalations through both nostrils, like a blacksmith's bellows. This generated internal heat and felt like a powerful energetic cleanse.
- **Kapalabhati (Skull Shining Breath):**
  - o **Purpose:** Purifying nadis, activating **Agni** (digestive fire), clearing the mind, promoting focus and mental sharpness.
  - o **How to Perform:** Similar to Bhastrika, but emphasizing short, sharp, active exhalations with passive inhalations, driven by the abdominal muscles. This felt like a rapid mental purification, bringing intense clarity.
- **Brahmari (Bumblebee Breath):**
  - o **Purpose:** Calming the mind, soothing the nervous system, reducing stress and anxiety.
  - o **How to Perform:** I'd inhale deeply, then on the exhale, make a low-pitched humming sound like a bumblebee, with my lips sealed and fingers gently pressing on my ear cartilage. This resonated deeply, providing internal calm.

Advanced Pranayama Techniques: Ascending to Greater Mastery

Higher on Prana Mountain, where the air was crisp and the views expansive, I encountered a select group of "Ascended Yogis". These practitioners had dedicated themselves to levels of mastery, embodied in techniques that demanded immense breath control, concentration, and energetic awareness. Observing them, and with careful guidance, I began to comprehend the depth of transformation these advanced Pranayamas offered. They spoke of these as gateways to deeper states of awareness, requiring not just vital energy but a fearless mind and unwavering concentration.

- **Surya Bhedana (Sun-Piercing Breath):**
  - o **Purpose:** Energizing, stimulating solar (Pingala) energy, awakening metabolism.
  - o **How to Perform (with guidance):** Inhaling only through the right nostril and exhaling only through the left.
  - o **Significance:** This technique embodies directed energy, boosting vitality and mental alertness.
- **Chandra Bhedana (Moon-Piercing Breath):**
  - o **Purpose**: Calming, cooling, balancing lunar(Ida) energy, promoting relaxation.
  - o **How to Perform (with guidance):** Inhaling only through the left nostril and exhaling only through the right.
  - o **Significance:** It embodies soothing energy, calming the nervous system and preparing for introspection.
- **Murchha (Fainting Breath):**
  - o **Purpose:** Inducing deep states of relaxation, withdrawal of the mind.
  - o **How to Perform (requires significant preparation and a guru):** This advanced technique involves a slow, deep inhalation followed by a prolonged retention with internal focus and as such should be practiced with caution under supervision by a teacher.

o **Significance:** It is known for its ability to quickly calm the mind and prepare for meditation, embodying a surrender of the outer world.

These advanced practices, I understood, were not destinations to be rushed, but techniques to be approached with reverence, patience, and a deep understanding of one's own energetic system and its readiness. They were the ultimate expression of **"Pranayama"** at its most demanding and transformative.

Adapting Pranayama: Breath for Everyday Life and Conditions

One of the most valuable lessons I learned on Prana Mountain was the adaptability of the practice. For those with stress, anxiety, or specific health conditions, many of these powerful Pranayama techniques can be modified and integrated into daily life, even while sitting or performing simple tasks. This opened up the practice to everyone, reinforcing that the essence of Pranayama is not rigid adherence, but the steady and comfortable experience of vital energy. For example, simple mindful breathing, akin to chair yoga for Asanas, can be done almost anywhere:

- **Conscious Abdominal Breathing:** Sitting comfortably, place one hand on your chest and one on your belly. Inhale deeply, feeling your belly rise first, then your chest. Exhale slowly, feeling your belly fall. This is a foundational practice for stress reduction.
- **Counting Breaths:** Simply counting your breaths (e.g., inhale for 4, hold for 2, exhale for 6) helps focus the mind and regulate the nervous system. This is a quiet, internal way to calm the mind in any situation.

- **Humming on Exhale:** A gentle humming sound on the exhale can be done quietly and discreetly to calm the mind and soothe the nervous system, a variation of Brahmari.

These modifications proved that the spirit of Pranayama—the cultivation of stability and ease in our energetic body—is accessible to all, regardless of physical or external circumstances.

The Master Practice: The Conscious Breath Cycle

Finally, I encountered what I came to call the Master Practice of Prana Mountain: the conscious manipulation of the complete breath cycle. This isn't a single technique, but the fundamental structure that underpins all Pranayama. It involves a precise awareness and control over the three core stages:

- **Puraka (Inhalation):** The conscious act of drawing prana into the body. This is more than just filling the lungs; it's about drawing in vital, life-giving energy.

- **Kumbhaka (Retention):** Holding the breath to assimilate and distribute prana throughout the entire system. This is the moment of stillness where energy permeates every cell.

- **Rechaka (Exhalation):** The conscious process of releasing prana and eliminating toxins. This is not just expelling air, but letting go of physical, mental, and emotional impurities.

This rhythmic cycle, when consciously controlled, became a miniature journey through the entire Prana Mountain, preparing me for the next stages of my allegorical climb by purifying my energetic being.

Yoga-Nidra: The Deep Rest Beyond Breath

During my climb, I came across a serene grove where a group of yogis lay motionless beneath the shade of ancient trees. Their faces radiated peace, their breath barely perceptible. I learned that they were practicing a method known as **Yoga-Nidra**, or "yogic sleep". They welcomed me into their circle and gently guided me through this deeply restorative practice. Unlike ordinary sleep, Yoga-Nidra invites awareness to remain alert in a state between waking and dreaming. Through guided breath, body awareness, and visualization, it allows access to the subconscious mind while the body is in complete rest. It provided a level of inner clarity and calm unlike anything I had previously experienced, acting as a bridge between breathwork and the deeper meditative states that lay ahead.

- **Purpose:**
  To induce deep relaxation, reduce stress, access the subconscious, and support emotional and physical restoration.

- **How to Perform:**
  Lie on your back in Shavasana, eyes closed and body fully relaxed. Set a Sankalpa (a short, positive intention like "I am calm."). Gently rotate awareness through the body, part by part, without movement. Then observe the natural breath. Visualizations or simple opposites (like warmth/coolness) may be introduced. After 10–30 minutes, return to body awareness and mentally restate your intention before rising.

- **Significance:**

A powerful practice for calming the mind, enhancing inner clarity, and restoring balance—especially useful for beginners or those with anxiety or insomnia. It complements Pranayama by fostering deeper states of rest and awareness.

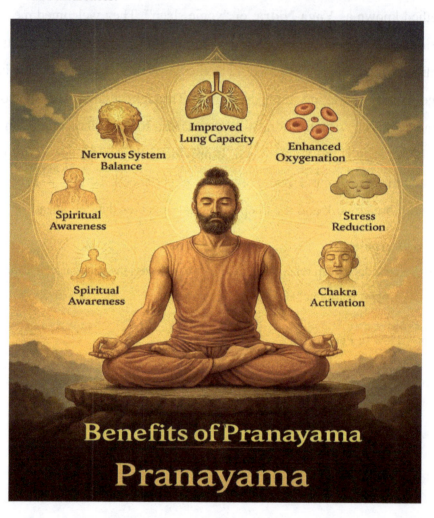

Benefits of Pranayama

Pranayama

Descending with Wisdom: Lessons Learned from Prana Mountain

My journey up Prana Mountain and the conversations with the Yogis I met left me with insights. These are the takeaway lessons I carry with me, not just for my breathing practice, but for my life:

- **Breath is Life, Conscious Breath is Control:** Pranayama taught me that our breath is our constant companion, and by becoming conscious of it, we gain a powerful tool for self-regulation. *"Shvasa eva jivam"* (breath is life!) echoed in my mind.

- **Balance is Key: The Power of Asymmetry:** Just as the nadis (Ida and Pingala) need to be balanced, so does our daily life. Pranayama teaches us to harmonize our active and receptive energies, leading to emotional stability (samata). The dynamic interplay of asymmetrical forces creates powerful harmony, as seen in the OM mantra.

- **Purification is a Prerequisite:** The cleansing aspect of Pranayama (*sharira shuddhi, nadi shuddhi*) is vital. Clearing internal blockages, whether physical or energetic, prepares the ground for deeper meditative states.

- **Mind Follows Breath:** The direct link between breath and mind (*mano nirodha*) became undeniable. By controlling the breath, I could calm the incessant chatter of the mind, leading to enhanced focus (*ekagrata*).

- **Patience and Consistency:** Like any climb, mastery of Pranayama requires consistent, gentle effort. Small, regular practices yield far greater results than infrequent, overly ambitious sessions.

- **Energetic Health is Foundational:** The subtle body and its energy channels are as crucial as the physical body. Pranayama allows us to directly influence this energetic realm for overall well-being.

Helpful Hints for Beginners and Those with Conditions

For those just beginning their climb of Prana Mountain, or for those navigating specific conditions like anxiety, stress, or certain respiratory issues, I offer these hard-won hints to ensure a safe, fulfilling, and beneficial journey:

- **Consult a Professional:** Always consult a qualified healthcare professional (knowing yoga techniques) before starting any new breathing regimen, especially if you have existing respiratory conditions (e.g., severe asthma, COPD), heart conditions, or high blood pressure. They may advise on safe and beneficial techniques.
- **Find a Qualified Teacher:** Seek out a yoga instructor who is experienced and knowledgeable in Pranayama, particularly one who understands contraindications and can offer modifications. A good teacher will emphasize safety and individual needs over forcing students into advanced techniques.
- **Never Force the Breath:** This is perhaps the most crucial lesson on Prana Mountain. Never push into strain or discomfort. If your breath feels forced or you become dizzy, ease off, adjust, or stop. Your body and energy are communicating; listen intently.
- **Embrace Gentleness and Patience:** Pranayama is a subtle practice. Don't view slower progress as a sign of weakness. It's a sign of intelligence and self-awareness. Gradual progression is key to long-term benefits and avoiding overstimulation.

- **Focus on the Exhale:** Often, the quality of your exhale dictates the quality of your inhale. Emphasize a full, relaxed exhalation to create space for a natural, deep inhale.
- **Consistency is Key:** Short, regular practices (even 5-10 minutes daily) are far more beneficial than sporadic, intense ones. Daily engagement with the breath builds energetic resilience.
- **Integrate into Daily Life:** Use simple breath awareness or techniques like conscious abdominal breathing during stressful moments, before sleep, or to improve focus during tasks. This is your daily *dinacharya* with breath.

Pranayama vs. Modern Breathing Exercises: A Comparative Look

As I considered the diverse paths to breath mastery, I couldn't help but compare the journey up Prana Mountain to the various modern breathing exercises advocated today. Both offer significant benefits, but their philosophies and ultimate outcomes differ considerably. Modern breathing exercises, often found in stress management, sports training, or clinical settings, typically focus on physiological outcomes: lowering heart rate, improving lung capacity, calming the nervous system, or enhancing athletic performance. They are often prescriptive, designed for specific, measurable results, and may utilize tools like biofeedback. While highly effective for their stated goals, they often view the breath primarily as a mechanical or physiological function, but lack a holistic understanding. Pranayama, on the other hand, offers a more perceptive approach, integrating mind, body, and the subtle energy (Prana) itself. While it certainly yields physiological benefits like improved lung function and stress reduction, its ultimate aim is coordinated development beyond material life: to purify the nadis, balance the vayus, quiet the mind (mano nirodha), and prepare the practitioner for deeper states of meditation and ultimately, self-realization. The emphasis is on conscious engagement with the life force, using breath as a tool for inner transformation rather than just physiological optimization. It acknowledges the breath's connection to consciousness. Ultimately, both paths have their merits, and some find great benefit in combining aspects of both, using yogic Pranayama to deepen the effects and understanding of more targeted breathing exercises.

The Future of Pranayama: A Vision for Wellness and Consciousness

Beyond individual well-being, I also came to realize Pranayama possesses immense, untapped potential, particularly within the realm of holistic health and consciousness studies. With further research and experimental approaches, these ancient practices could be more fully integrated into therapeutic regimes for a wide range of conditions. Their focus on regulating the autonomic nervous system, purifying energetic channels, and calming the mind is precisely what is needed to address many chronic conditions, from stress-related disorders and anxiety to respiratory ailments and even neurological imbalances.

The application of specific Pranayama techniques extends to the management of respiratory diseases and dysfunctions (e.g., asthma, COPD) and wider systemic pathologies, drawing from scientific literature (e.g., PubMed reviews) and traditional yogic texts. Moreover, the emphasis on conscious breath and inner focus could significantly help to combat mental fog and enhance cognitive function in an increasingly distracted world. By fostering mental resilience, emotional balance, and aiding in efficient energetic recovery, Pranayama could play a crucial role in extending and increasing the quality of life, allowing individuals to live with greater vitality and clarity. This vision of incorporating Pranayama as a fundamental pillar of wellness and consciousness development excites me greatly.

My journey on Prana Mountain revealed that true energetic mastery isn't about rigid breath control alone, but about the relationship we cultivate with our own vital life force. It's about finding that sweet spot of effort and ease in the breath, listening to the subtle language of our energetic body, and respecting its wisdom. With this newfound vitality and clarity forged in the crucible of Pranayama, I feel better prepared to face the next challenges on the Mountain of Yoga—the enigmatic River of Pratyahara that lies ahead, a crucial step in turning the senses inward.

Conclusion: The Transformative Power of Breath

As I look back from the summit of Prana Mountain, it is clear to me that this disciplined yet gentle approach to energetic well-being deserves wider practice and recognition. In a world that often values external results and intense exertion, Pranayama offers a path to sustainable energy, inner calm, and a deep connection between breath, mind, and spirit. They are not just breathing exercises; they are a means to cultivate energetic resilience, mental peace, and self-awareness that transcends the yoga mat and enriches every aspect of life. This life-force regime is a timeless gift, accessible to all, and its holistic benefits make it an invaluable pursuit for anyone seeking a deeper, more integrated approach to living.

River of Sensory Dissonance (River Pratyahara)

We gathered at the river's edge, a small band of yogis, staring at the scary scene before us. This was the River of Distraction, its roar a palpable challenge. A cold knot of doubt tightened in our stomachs. Were we truly ready for what lay across? The wind, already fierce, seemed to amplify our nervousness.

Before us stretched a bridge, ancient and formidable, its old timbers groaning, a skeletal pathway swaying violently with every powerful gust. We watched, mesmerized by its dangerous dance. Frayed ropes, our precarious lifeline, whipped like angry serpents, our only visible link to the other side. This sight alone declared the true nature of the test ahead. Yet, a quiet resolve began to settle within us. We exchanged silent glances, a collective decision forming. With a shared breath, a leap of faith, we stepped onto the old structure. Each step was slow, deliberate, our eyes fixed on the slippery planks and unstable ropes, searching for the slightest firm hold.

The wind was relentless. Each blast threatened to dislodge our foothold, to sweep us into the churning depths. We learned to pause, to wait out the worst of its fury, steadying ourselves before venturing onward. The ropes groaned, threatening to snap. We knew, deep down, that a fall here was more than a physical plunge. It was a spiritual and moral collapse. It meant beginning our entire journey anew, back at the Yamas. This was the ultimate test of our inner purity and faith.

Looking down from the swaying bridge intensified the terror. The river below was a churning, white-capped monster, a blur of ragged rapids and dark, jagged rocks spinning relentlessly. The sheer power of the water pulled at our minds, a dizzying, relentless force. From this height, we felt tiny, insignificant, about to be swallowed by the roaring chaos. The deafening roar beneath was a constant, stark reminder of the danger.

We understood clearly the consequences of such a fall. It wasn't merely pain; it was a deeper failure. We would be swept away by the very distractions we sought to transcend. All the discipline and self-control forged through the Yamas and Niyamas would unravel. It would demand a complete restart of our spiritual path, a humbling return to square one. We recalled the sage Vishwamitra, who, in his pursuit of Brahmarishi status like Vashistha, repeatedly saw his intense penance broken by distractions, be it celestial nymphs or his own anger. Each time, he had to gather himself, acknowledge his lapse, and begin his arduous journey anew, underlining his immense, unwavering focus required for such a path.

With this renewed understanding, a quiet determination settled within. We summoned our collective will, our gazes firm, and with a silent prayer for strength, we pushed forward. This perilous crossing, we understood, embodied the very essence of Pratyahara. Patanjali, in his Yoga Sutras, defines the fifth limb of yoga, Pratyahara, with the following:

स्वविषयासंप्रयोगे चित्तस्य स्वरूपानुकारः इव इन्द्रियाणां प्रत्याहारः।

(Sva viṣaya asaṁprayoge cittasya svarūpānukāraḥ iva indriyāṇām pratyāhāraḥ)

This sutra conveys that when the mind, or citta, withdraws from its engagement with external objects, and the senses, or indriyas, follow by turning inward and reflecting the inner nature of the mind, that state is known as Pratyahara, the conscious withdrawal of the senses from their respective sense objects.

The "River of Distraction" and its sensory assault represent the constant influx of external stimuli. Our senses – eyes, ears, skin – naturally reach outward, connecting with their objects. Pratyahara is about consciously severing this connection. It is the mind (citta), habitually drawn to external stimuli, learning to detach. When the mind succeeds, our senses (indriyas), acting as obedient instruments, "follow suit". They cease their outward

87

search and turn inward. This isn't about ignoring the world but about freeing ourselves from its compulsive pull. It's as if our senses, no longer commanded by a wandering mind, pivot from the terrifying river back towards the inner sanctuary.

Our actions on that bridge were not solely physical; they were governed by the totality of our being. Within us lies a clear hierarchy at its apex, our discriminative intellect (Buddhi). This was the part that knew the bridge's danger, understood the stakes of falling, and recognized the absolute necessity of focus. Our Buddhi had to guide and command our mind—the seat of thoughts and emotions—to remain steadfast, to quell panic, to disregard the overwhelming sights and sounds. The mind, in turn, controlled our physical expressions: the careful locomotion of our limbs, the precise focus of our sensory organs. Even our fear-driven emotions had to be disciplined, ensuring our will remained resolute. Every deliberate step, every pause for balance, was a challenge to Buddhi's power to direct the mind, and the mind's capacity to guide our faculties despite the external chaos.

The Task of Crossing: Pratyahara in Action

As we continued our precarious crossing, the true challenge of Pratyahara materialized. The roaring river, the biting wind, the swaying bridge—these were the constant pulls on our senses, the "objects" (visaya) of Patanjali's teaching. Our eyes yearned to fixate on the dizzying rapids, our ears to dwell on the wind's howl, our bodies to react purely from fear. Yet, our task was to consciously prevent our mind (citta) from forging these

88

connections with external stimuli. It was a deliberate act of internal redirection. We were not ignoring the dangers; our Buddhi remained keenly aware. But our focus fundamentally shifted. Instead of letting the external chaos scatter our senses, we actively pulled them inward. Our gaze softened, perceiving the bridge as a precise path, not a terrifying abyss. The wind's roar became background, not a call to panic. Each movement was a calculated act of discipline, our limbs responding not to external threats but to the calm, clear instructions from our inner awareness. This was the continuous practice of Pratyahara: ensuring our senses, rather than being dispersed by the world, remained tethered to our central purpose and the unwavering guidance of our higher intellect. Slowly, arduously, we pressed on. We passed the halfway mark, and with each new step, the difficulty only escalated. It was a stark echo of the ancient adage: the spiritual path truly resembled walking on a razor's edge. We summoned every last vestige of energy, every fiber of our will, to push through. The end of the bridge finally came into view, but a new test awaited. A heavy mist obscured the final few rungs, revealing only a single, inviting landing platform just beyond the last, invisible step. From this platform, the initial steps leading into the mouth of a tunnel were clearly visible, marking the passage to climb the next mountain of Dharana. Once more, hesitation crept in. Could we truly take that final leap of faith, a blind jump from an unseen rung onto a solid stone platform, trusting it would hold?

Then, through the swirling mist, two figures appeared. They stood on the very first step of the tunnel climb, senior yogis clad in pristine white, seeming to shimmer with an unearthly glow. They raised their hands in a gesture of welcome and encouragement, beckoning us to jump, one by one. Their serene presence brought an immediate wave of relief and reassurance. With mounting excitement, we gathered our courage. One by one, we took that leap of faith into the unseen, landing safely on the solid platform with the strong, guiding hands of the waiting yogis. Even in the cold wind, our faces were warm, sweating, our eyes moist with tears of pure, intense joy. We had crossed the fearful river. We had left the material world of toil and trouble behind, now poised at the threshold of the serene, spiritual world.

The Meaning of the Crossing and the Path Ahead

With gratitude in our hearts, we sank onto the inviting steps at the suggestion of our heavenly guides. Their presence was a balm after the chaotic crossing. In voices as clear and soothing as a mountain spring, our mentors began to elucidate the entire meaning of our arduous journey. They clarified the 'how' and 'why' of Pratyahara: When our senses relentlessly seek external gratification or react to outside stimuli, our mind (citta) remains agitated and fragmented. Pratyahara is the crucial step that gathers this scattered energy, bringing the senses back under the command of a focused mind, which itself is guided by the discerning intellect (Buddhi). This internal mastery, they emphasized, is absolutely necessary for the deeper stages of meditation. Without it, our minds would forever be pulled back to the 'river of distraction', unable to sustain focus. Our guides then illuminated the promise that lay ahead beyond this gateway. The serene landing platform and the inviting steps into the tunnel marked our transition. We had left behind the material world of toil and trouble, a realm where our senses perpetually demand attention, pulling us away from our true selves. We were now entering a space of divine serenity, where genuine inner exploration could commence.

This tunnel, they revealed, was our passage to the next mountain: Dharana. If Pratyahara was the courageous act of withdrawing the senses, Dharana, they explained, was the discipline of holding that focus. It means concentrating the mind on a single point—a sound, an image, a breath, or an idea—without wavering. They warned that this new challenge would demand maintaining an unbroken flow of attention, resisting even the subtle attempts of the mind to drift, now without the overwhelming external distractions. It was the essential training ground for unwavering stillness.

It is through this sustained focus of Dharana, they concluded, that one prepares for the depths of Dhyana, the meditative state where the distinction between meditator and object begins to dissolve. And beyond Dhyana, like a rarely climbed peak, lay Samadhi, the ultimate union, a state of complete absorption and enlightenment. Pratyahara, they impressed upon us, is the foundational courage to cross that initial terrifying river, making the subsequent climb possible. It is the vital key that unlocks the deeper, rarely scaled mountains of the meditative journey, leading ultimately to true liberation. We stood ready, refreshed, and eager for these new adventures.

Mount of Focus (Dharanadri)

The Landscape of Clarity

Before me stretched Mount Dharana, a panorama of astounding clarity and incisive focus. There was nothing fuzzy or ambiguous here; the very air seemed to vibrate with precision. Every contour, every distant peak, every subtle shade of rock and foliage was defined with an almost impossible sharpness. It was clarity personified, a landscape that demanded and mirrored absolute attention. As I ascended the initial steps of the footpath, I encountered a group of yogis, their faces serene yet intensely concentrated. They were engaged in a lively discussion, their voices carrying on the pure mountain air, centered on the very essence of this realm: how to attain focus as piercing and unwavering as a laser. One yogi, with captivating storytelling, began to illustrate this singular focus with a vivid narration from the Mahabharata. He recounted the famous arrow-shooting contest where Drona, the teacher of the Kauravas and Pandavas, challenged his disciples to hit the painted eye of a distant wooden bird mounted on a low-hanging tree branch. "Many of Drona's disciples failed," he explained, "unable to fix their minds on the target. Then, Drona called his favorite student, Arjuna, and asked him to take aim." The yogi's voice deepened as he continued, "Drona asked Arjuna, 'What do you see?' Arjuna replied, 'I see the bird's head.' Drona urged him to focus further on the target. 'What do you see now?' Drona pressed. Arjuna's voice, in the yogi's telling, became a whisper of pure concentration, 'The center of the black eye of the bird.' Drona exclaimed, 'Good! Now shoot!' And the arrow, true to its aim, found its mark, to the thunderous applause of all present."

The yogi concluded, his gaze sweeping over us, "The trick, Drona revealed, is to shrink the field of your vision, to pinpoint the object in your mind until nothing but the core of an object, or a subject, or a concept you are trying to comprehend remains. This process, this act of sustained, unwavering of the mind, of course, within the perspective of the whole act, has a name. It is called Dharana. This laser like focus is precisely what Patanjali defined as Dharana."

देशबन्धश्चित्तस्य धारणा ॥

deśa-bandhaś cittasya dhāraṇā

"Dhāraṇā is the binding (bandhaḥ) of the mind (cittasya) to one place (deśa)."

The Ascent of Mental Refinement

With the story of Arjuna's focus resonating in my mind, I began the ascent of Mount Dharana. The climb itself was a journey of gradual refinement. The winding pathways were punctuated by serene, crystal-clear contemplative pond areas, each one offering unique opportunities to learn the nuanced means and techniques of cultivating that laser-like focus. Here, under the watchful eyes of experienced yogis, we would engage in practices designed to hone our minds, to systematically cut all mental clutter that had accumulated from a lifetime of external distractions. The goal was not just to concentrate, but to truly sharpen our mental processes for critical, discriminative intellect, sculpting our awareness into a singular, penetrating laser beam.

The air itself felt conducive to such clarity, enabling concentrated efforts of countless seekers who had walked these very paths, leaving behind an energetic imprint of growing mental discipline.

The Summit of Inquiry

Finally, after climbing a steep ascent of the footpath – each step a challenge in concentrated mobilization of my strength, stamina, and courage – I reached the summit. Here, on a wide, open plateau, a discussion on Dharana was about to begin. The platform itself, sculpted with precision from a smooth, cool marble, boasted four seats of natural stone, each glowing with an aura of clarity. Below, the audience, some fifteen persons, were comfortably seated on rough-hewn stone chairs. On the platform, two women and two men formed the thought leaders, symbolizing, I mused, the

94

unity of Prakriti and Purusha, or perhaps the synthesis of the right and left sides of the human brain — the emotional and the intellectual brought into harmony. Nothing looked artificial here; everything seemed to belong to nature. Around us, silent water fountains at the edge of the clearing added a delicate beauty and symmetry to the proceedings. After a short, resonant Shanti Mantra, the seminar, if I can call it that, began.

A yogini, her presence radiating a calm and piercing intellect, was the first to speak. She explained that Dharana is the high point of both intellectual and emotional focus on an object or thought, a paradigm, a phenomenon, or a natural law. "It follows what could be called a spiral pathway," she articulated, her voice clear and precise, "going on an inward, circular journey from infinity to a point which literally has a position but no dimension. The Upanishadic wisdom describes it beautifully as Anoraniyan Mahato Mahiyan – smaller than the smallest, greater than the greatest. While this point is the ultimate end, it is evident at every stage, whether inwards or outwards; the other end extends into infinity. And at every stage, the circumscribed thought is never without perspective." Her eyes swept across the eager faces in the audience. "This is the point we reach after another climb, through meditation, to the three OM states in Samadhi. Learn it and you will know yourself, and your Karma, and your Antaryami or Internal Divinity." The watchwords, she seemed to convey, were indeed FOCUS and Perspective – an inextricable duality shaping the unity of thought and action.

A yogi in the audience, who must have been a research scientist in the material world we had left behind, raised his finger to ask a question. His voice, though respectful, carried the keen analytical edge of his former discipline. "Yogini," he began, "what you spoke is truly enlightening. In the yonder material world, which we left behind, we often focus without perspective and call it super-specialization. And throughout humanity's ascent, through disparate disciplines, science and technology have advanced tremendously in one sense and brought a level of unprecedented material comforts. Yet, this has also gradually weakened its enduring base and created some major crises, which in our era are coalescing as existential threats, threatening our very survival. We see it in every walk of life: we have now inequality and a growing divide between the rich and the poor, distrust between nations, the climate crisis, loss of environment, and our latest marvels – machine learning and artificial intelligence – have proven instances of misuse which, if left unchecked, threaten our very independence and existence. My question is, how do we restore the perspective to focus and translate it into sustainable development of human ascent?"

The yogis on the dais looked at each other, a silent acknowledgment passing between them. Then, the yogi in the middle, who appeared to be the oldest and wisest of the group, gently nodded and took the question. His gaze settled on the former scientist, his eyes reflecting compassion and understanding. "Your analysis of the situation is clear and valid, my friend," the elder yogi began, his voice calm yet resonating with ancient wisdom. "Indeed, the material world, in its pursuit of fragmented knowledge, often cultivates a focus that is devoid of perspective. This super specialization, as you rightly term it, isolates disciplines and endeavors, severing their connection to the greater whole. When a part operates without awareness of its relationship to the complete system, imbalance is inevitable."

He continued, "The crises you enumerate – inequality, distrust, environmental degradation, the misuse of powerful technologies like AI – are not failures of intellect or capacity. They are, fundamentally, failures of perspective. When our focus narrows to the immediate, the tangible, the self-serving, without acknowledging the intricate web of interdependence, we inadvertently create discord. We focus on maximizing profit without the perspective of ecological impact, on technological advancement without the perspective of human flourishing and ethical implications, and on individual gain without the perspective of collective well-being. This is precisely the realm we just transcended with Pratyahara – the domain where the senses, and by extension the mind, are constantly pulled outwards, fragmenting our awareness. So, how do we restore perspective to focus and translate it into sustainable human ascent? The answer lies in the very essence of Dharana itself. Arjuna's story, which our sister yogini shared, illustrates this perfectly. His focus on the bird's eye was not a blind, isolated fixation. It was a sharpening, a cutting through all superficial distractions, to perceive the essence of his target. And in that ultimate clarity of the essence, lies the universal connection."

The yogi leaned slightly forward, his eyes twinkling. "True Dharana is not merely concentrating on a point; it is concentrating into a point, realizing that this point, as the Upanishads say, is Anoraniyan Mahato Mahiyan – smaller than the smallest, yet containing the greatness of the greatest. When your mind achieves such singular focus on an object, a concept, or even your own breath, it doesn't just narrow; it deepens. It penetrates the surface, revealing the interconnectedness that was always there, though obscured by mental clutter. This focus, imbued with innate perspective, transforms our actions. If a scientist, through Dharana, focuses on the climate crisis with the understanding that humanity is an integral part of the planet, not separate from it, their solutions will naturally be holistic and sustainable. If a leader focuses on governance with the deep realization of the shared Antaryami (Inner-Self) within every individual, then policies will inherently move towards equality and justice, bridging divides rather than widening them. If creators of AI cultivate this deep focus on the nature of consciousness and human values, their creations will serve humanity's true ascent, rather than threaten its essence."

The elder yogi paused, his gaze sweeping over the audience, acknowledging the gravity of the scientist's observations. "My friend, you speak of the headwinds of human nature, of lands exceeding their carrying capacity, of destruction's pace, and of forces of dystopia that seem more powerful than the voices of sustainable development. You suggest we may have reached a point of no return. Yet, we must persevere. While the challenges are immense, and the path arduous, more and more people need to take this enlightening path." His voice gained a quiet strength, a resolve. "The efforts to preserve this ancient path of Yoga, to protect and nurture this precious spark of wisdom, must continue, for it holds the potential to ignite a conflagration when the right moment, when the right call, comes. This is important for all of us. When the time is right, all of us who have walked this path, who have tasted this clarity, will return to carry the torch.

We will fight against the collective ego, against pervasive greed, against the turbulent energies of Rajas and the inertia of Tamas, against hate and against ignorance itself. That, my friends, is the ultimate call of the Supreme Power. Life and time run in cycles. All we have to believe in is this eternal truth: if winter comes, can spring be far behind?"

Descent and Take-Home Lessons: Cultivating Focus for Meditation

The scene changed, and I found myself descending the pathways of Mount Dharana, my mind overflowing with the insights shared at the summit. The ascent and the wisdom absorbed had transformed my understanding, not just of focus, but of its essential interplay with perspective.

This was not merely theoretical knowledge; it was a blueprint for action, for approaching the next, penultimate mountain of meditation. My take-home lessons and practical steps for cultivating this refined focus for meditation, or Dhyana, were clear:

- Embrace the Spiral of Deepening Focus: Just as the yogini described, Dharana is an inward spiral. It's not about forcing the mind to concentrate but gently guiding it. Begin with a broader object of focus – perhaps the breath, a mantra, or a visual image. Then, gradually, with sustained attention, allow your awareness to deepen and narrow, much like Arjuna narrowing his sight from the bird's head to its eye. The initial object provides a starting point; the deepening process cultivates true Dharana.

- Confront and Clear Mental Clutter (Mini Pratyahara): The constant distractions of the material world, and even our own internal chatter, are the "frayed ropes" of the bridge we just crossed. Before attempting sustained focus, practice mini-Pratyahara sessions. Dedicate a few minutes each day to simply observing the flow of thoughts and sensations without judgment, allowing them to pass without attachment. This trains the mind to disengage from external and internal "noise," preparing it for the singular commitment of Dharana.

- Integrate Perspective with Every Focus: This was the crucial insight from the elder yogi. Whatever your object of focus in meditation, hold an underlying awareness of its interconnectedness. If you focus on a mantra, feel its vibration resonate through your entire being and beyond. If you focus on your heart chakra, sense its connection to universal love and compassion. This ensures your focus is not isolated but is a gateway to expansive perspective, preventing the spiritual "super-specialization" that can lead to imbalance.

- Dharma as the Guiding Light: The existential threats highlighted by the scientist resonated deeply. Applying Dharana to our daily lives means aligning our focus with our Dharma, our righteous duty and purpose. Every task, every interaction, can become an exercise in focused action with a broader perspective of contribution and harmony. This is the practical application of spiritual insight to sustainable human ascent.

- Patience and Perseverance: The climb up Mount Dharana, like any spiritual endeavor, requires immense patience. There will be headwinds, moments when the mind wanders, or the focus wavers. But the yogi's final words about the cycles of life and the coming of spring were a powerful reminder: the spark, once lit, must be protected and nurtured. Consistent, gentle effort, even when progress seems slow, is key. Each moment of truly engaged focus builds the mental muscle needed for deeper states of meditation.

The technological revolution, marked by spectacular advancements like artificial intelligence and machine learning, has undeniably propelled humankind forward. Yet, ironically, these very advancements hold the seeds of humanity's escalating existential dilemmas. We've touched upon one critical flaw: development has become imbalanced, lacking a vital sense of perspective. This missing perspective lies at the root of the dystopia we increasingly face. What we often forget is that this narrow perspective fails to encompass the very purpose of these inventions. Why, for instance, do we pursue AI? Ostensibly, to increase human comfort and wealth. Herein lies the embedded snare: greed, manifesting in the rapidly widening chasm between the rich and the poor, becomes the underlying driver. To resolve these existential problems, our perspective must return to fundamental principles. We must clearly and unequivocally align the purpose of all human progress not with the mere accumulation of material possessions, wealth, or comfort, but with a far grander vision. This renewed purpose must encompass human enlightenment, a deeper understanding of self and beyond, the holistic well-being of the planet, the preservation of nature, the cultivation of empathy and love, and respect for all living creatures and the environment. If our innovations spring from these deep roots of an all-encompassing perspective, the existential challenges confronting humanity will begin to dissolve, paving the way for a truly harmonious and flourishing future. With these lessons firmly etched in my consciousness, I felt a renewed sense of purpose. The next climb, the path to Dhyana (meditation), seemed less daunting, more attainable, now that I understood the true nature of the focused mind.

Mount of Meditation (Dhyanadri)

The crisp mountain air invigorated me as I stepped onto the path, leaving behind the mundane. This wasn't merely a physical climb; it was an inner expedition, an ascent towards the "penultimate peak of Meditation," the doorway to ultimate bliss and reality. My fellow yoga practitioners, a small group of earnest seekers, gathered around me. Their faces reflected a quiet determination, a shared purpose to embark on something profound. The air hummed with an almost imperceptible vibration, the collective intent, beckoning us forward.

Our guides, a venerable Yogi and a serene Yogini, sat poised in the center of our semi-circle. The Yogi radiated calm authority, while the Yogini embodied a gentle wisdom, their eyes holding the deep insight of those who have traversed these peaks countless times. A simple yet elegant diagram rested beside them, hinting at the subtle stages of the inner landscape we were about to explore.

"Welcome, earnest seekers," the Yogi began, his voice resonant and clear, his gaze sweeping over each of us. The Yogini added, her voice soft yet firm, "You stand at the threshold of Dhyana, the peak of Meditation. This is not merely a practice; it is a state of being, a journey from the many to the One, from the transient to the eternal. Our climb here will challenge your perceptions, refine your awareness, and ultimately, open the doorway to that ultimate bliss, that ultimate reality you yearn for."

They gestured towards the peak rising majestically above us, its summit often veiled in mists, symbolizing the subtle, often elusive nature of true meditative states. "This peak, unlike a sheer rock face," the Yogini explained, "reveals itself through a series of curves and levels. It's a zig-zagging path with visible stops near pretty ponds and natural benches in the shade. These ponds signify moments of deepening stillness and reflection, where consciousness settles to reflect reality without distortion. The shaded benches offer rest and integration, allowing us to consolidate learning and adapt to new levels of awareness. True progress in meditation involves a rhythm of focused engagement and restful assimilation." The Yogi clarified the scope of Meditation, emphasizing it's more than just concentration or relaxation:

1. **Moving Beyond Mere Concentration:** Meditation is the **uninterrupted flow of focused attention**, effortlessly illuminating the object without wavering.

2. **Transcending the Object:** The initial object of focus becomes a **doorway** to move beyond surface mental layers, quieting thought-waves to allow deeper awareness.

3. **Cultivating Inner Stillness (Nirodha):** The aim is a state of stillness where mental fluctuations cease, revealing a rich, aware silence.

4. **Awakening Intuition and Insight:** As the mind settles, direct knowing (*prajna*) arises, leading to insights into reality beyond intellectual understanding.

5. **Dissolving the Sense of 'I' (Ego):** The ultimate goal is to soften and dissolve the limited sense of self, realizing the true Self (**Atman**) and experiencing oneness with Universal Consciousness.

We then discussed the "hard questions" that would become the very subjects of our meditation: "Who am I?", "What is the purpose of life?",

104

"What propels me and inspires me towards this ultimate climb?", "What is Karma?", "What is my relationship with my inner divinity or Antaryami? How can I open the door to Universal Consciousness?", and "What is the ultimate destiny of evolving life?" These are not intellectual puzzles but portals to direct experience.

Regarding the modalities for this climb, the Yogini explained:

- **Focused Attention (Samatha/Concentration-based):** Such as Mantra Meditation, Breath Awareness, Trataka, Japa Yoga, and Saguna Dhyana.

- **Open Awareness / Insight (Vipassana/Mindfulness-based):** Observing phenomena without judgment to gain insight into reality.

- **Self-Inquiry (Jnana Yoga-based):** Direct investigation into the nature of the mind and self, ideal for the "hard questions".

- **Devotional Meditation (Bhakti Yoga-based):** Cultivating love and devotion towards a divine form.

The Yogi added that finding what suits one's being comes through experimentation and honest self-assessment, listening to inner experience. He stressed that Karma Yoga, the path of selfless action, serves as an invaluable preparation for this climb, purifying the mind and fostering the clarity needed for deeper meditative insights. "Indeed, many who embark on this inner climb find that the path of Karma Yoga, of selfless action performed without attachment to results, serves an invaluable preparation. It purifies the mind, reduces the burden of past impressions, and fosters the mental clarity and detachment necessary to truly engage with these ultimate questions in meditation, thereby accelerating the evolution towards our true destiny."

Patanjali's Yoga Sutra on Dhyana

As we acknowledged the guidance that had brought us to this point it was fitting to recall the foundational text that illuminates the path of Dhyana. Patanjali's Yoga Sutras provide a succinct and powerful definition:

तत्र प्रत्यय्यैकतानता ध्यानम् ॥२॥

Tatra pratyayaikatānatā dhyānam ||2||

"There, the continuity in depth of the same cognition (Dharna) is Dhyana (meditation)."

Explanation: This sutra, following the definition of Dharana (concentration), states that when the focused attention (*pratyaya*) remains unbroken and uninterrupted on the object, that continuous flow is **Dhyana**, or meditation. It's the seamless, effortless maintenance of awareness on a single point, without any breaks or shifts. If Dharana is holding the light steady, Dhyana is the unwavering illumination itself.

Our Group Climb: The Triangular Pond of the Gunas

With a return of our respectful bows and a gentle gesture from our guides, we began the climb. The path immediately fulfilled its promise of a zig-zagging ascent. Soon enough, it opened up, and we arrived at our first designated stop: a breathtaking, triangular-shaped clearing situated in the middle of a serene pond, dotted with vibrant water lilies and majestic lotus blossoms. The Yogi and Yogini settled gracefully, indicating for us to do the same. "Welcome to our first pond of reflection," the Yogini began, her voice a soft murmur that didn't disturb the peace. "This shape, the triangle, is representing the fundamental energies that shape our nature: the three Gunas – Sattva, Rajas, and Tamas." The Yogi continued, "These Gunas are born from the Pancha Mahabhutas and influence our minds and bodies." He elaborated on each:

- **Sattva (Purity, Harmony, Light):** Embodied by the clear, still water and pure lotus petals, it represents clarity, balance, peace, and wisdom – the state most conducive to meditation.
- **Rajas (Activity, Passion, Motion):** Seen in the subtle currents and the lotus pushing through mud, it signifies action, energy, and ambition, but can lead to restlessness if unchecked.
- **Tamas (Inertia, Darkness, Stasis):** Represented by the unseen mud and dense shade, it denotes inertia, dullness, and resistance, leading to lethargy if excessive.

"Our aim here," the Yogini concluded, "is to transcend their binding effects and cultivate a predominance of Sattva. As you observe the beauty around you, allow yourself to feel the presence of these Gunas within your own being. This awareness is the first step towards transcending their influence, aiding in our Sattva Sanchaya – the commendable accumulation of purity and reduction of the sleepwalking material, Rajas and the ugly reality of Tamas." We settled into the stillness, gazing at the lotus, consciously directing our awareness to observe the subtle interplay of these fundamental qualities within ourselves.

The Oval Pond: Purpose, Evolution, and Destiny

The path ahead then split into three intertwining footpaths. We instinctively followed one, guided by our inner nature, recognizing them as Bhakti Marga, Jnana Marga, and Karma Marga. These paths, though distinct, led us to our next stop: an oval-shaped pond. The gentle curve of its banks created a sense of contained infinity, and its surface, a deeper blue, reflected the vastness of the sky. We paused to rest and meditate here on the grand questions of existence. The Yogi and Yogini guided us. "At this tranquil point," the Yogini began, "we will focus on three interconnected inquiries, allowing them to resonate within our deepest consciousness, just as the sky reflects in this water:

1. **The Purpose of All Life:** What is the inherent meaning, the fundamental drive, behind the endless cycle of birth, growth, and dissolution across all forms of existence?

2. **The Meaning of Evolution:** Beyond biological adaptation, what is the spiritual or conscious trajectory of evolution?

3. **The Ultimate End Point (or Destiny):** Where is this grand cosmic journey ultimately leading?"

We employed the Pranayama technique with our gaze fixed at the tip of the nose (Nasikagra Drishti). My eyes softly closed, and my breath flowed regularly, allowing the questions to settle. I intuited that purpose isn't external, but an inherent quality of existence – a continuous unfolding towards greater awareness. Evolution felt like a deliberate process of refinement, revealing the eternal. The ultimate destiny is a merging back into the source, a state of pure, unbounded consciousness, where the concept of Ananda (bliss) becomes tangible.

Many in the group nodded in agreement, having perceived the same truth from their own unique perspectives, irrespective of the path they arrived by. This shared understanding was powerfully articulated as the identical outcome of both Sankhya and Yoga, a wisdom from the Bhagavad Gita. It solidified our realization that the diverse paths to truth ultimately converge on the same liberating insight.

The Circular Pool: Antaryami, Ultimate Reality, and Moksha Unified by our deep understanding, we moved onward. The path led us to a breathtaking clearing beside a cascading waterfall, plunging into a deep, serene circular pool. It's perfect, unending form symbolized the Universal Consciousness (Brahman), while the waterfall's flow represented existence's vibrant energy merging into peace. Smooth, naturally worn stones served as our seats. "Welcome to the abode of unity," the Yogi intoned. The Yogini continued, "Here, we arrive at the culmination of our inquiries, the final hard question that dissolves all others. We will now turn our purified awareness to the very core of our being, directly experiencing the ultimate truth. Our focus today is on the Divine Inner Entity (Antaryami)—that spark of the Divine within each of us—and its non-dual relationship to the Ultimate Reality. We are seeking to realize, not just understand, the nature of Moksha, Mukti, Nirvana, or Liberation—that state of unadulterated, pure Joy that is our true, unchanging home." Again, we applied the Nasikagra Drishti with regular, deep breathing. Hours passed in serene meditation. When we finally opened our eyes, an exquisite joy filled the clearing. Our faces radiated a shared peace of mind and enlightenment. When my turn came to share, my meditation enabled me to understand deeply what the Shvetashvatara Upanishad (6.11) so aptly describes (Quoted in Ishwar Pranidhan):

"एको देवः सर्वभूतेषुगूढः सर्वव्यापी सर्वभूतान्तरात्मा । कर्माध्यक्षः सर्वभूताधिवासःसाक्षी चेता केवलो निर्गुणश्च।।"

(Eko Devaḥ sarvabhu̅teṣu gu̅ḍhaḥ sarvavya̅pi̅ sarvabhu̅ta̅ntara̅tma̅ | Karma̅dhyakṣaḥ sarvabhu̅ta̅dhiva̅saḥ sa̅kṣi̅ ceta̅ kevalo nirguṇas'ca ||)

"There is but one mysterious Organizing Power, hidden in all beings, all-pervading, the inner Self of all beings, the enabler of all actions, residing in all beings, the witness, the pure consciousness, and devoid of all qualities."

The Yogi and Yogini elaborated: this verse speaks to the oneness of the divine (*Eko Devaḥ*), its immanence (*gūḍhaḥ*, hidden in all beings), its omnipresence (*sarvavyāpī*), and its identity as the inner Self of all beings (*sarvabhūtāntarātmā*), the very definition of Antaryami. It is the silent overseer of actions (*Karmādhyakṣaḥ*), the witness (*Sākṣī*), pure consciousness (*Chetā*), absolute and alone (*Kevalaḥ*), and crucially, transcending all qualities (*Nirguṇaś-ca*) – meaning beyond the Gunas (Sattva, Rajas, Tamas) and all conditioned attributes. This description resonated deeply with Einstein's appreciation for Spinoza's God – an impersonal, infinite, all-encompassing substance identical with Nature itself, the immanent cause of all things, not separate from creation. My meditation had allowed me to experience the very essence of this truth.

110

Our Individual Descent: Take-Home Lessons and Preparatory Advice

The Yogi and Yogini acknowledged our accomplishment, reminding us that the path to Samadhi and the OM state would now become deeply individual. They blessed us and bid us Godspeed. We descended individually, each step an integration of the wisdom gained.

Here are the take-home lessons from our extraordinary climb:

1. **Dhyana is Sustained Absorption, Not Mere Focus:** Meditation is the uninterrupted, effortless flow of awareness leading to deep absorption, transcending the effort of initial concentration.

2. **The "Hard Questions" are Gateways to Direct Experience:** Inquiries, when held in sustained awareness, unlock intuitive, experiential answers from within.

3. **Unity in Diversity of Paths:** Bhakti, Jnana, and Karma Marga, when pursued with sincerity, converge at the same peak of ultimate truth.

4. **The Gunas: Cultivate Sattva, Transcend Bindings:** Consciously discerning and cultivating Sattva (purity, clarity) while minimizing Rajas (restlessness) and Tamas (dullness) is a vital, continuous practice.

5. **Life's Purpose: Integrated Development:** Life's purpose is the continuous unfolding towards one's highest physical, mental, and spiritual potential, an evolutionary journey of refinement.

6. **Antaryami is Pure Joy and Ultimate Reality:** The Divine Inner Entity is the essence of Ultimate Reality—a state of unadulterated, pure Joy (Moksha/Nirvana/Liberation) that is ever-present and our true nature.

111

7. **The Equivalence of Sankhya and Yoga:** The Bhagavad Gita's wisdom affirms that diverse approaches to truth ultimately converge on the same liberating insight.

For those who will follow in our footsteps, preparing to embark on this magnificent climb of meditation, I offer the following useful advice on basic preparatory steps:

1. **Cultivate an Ethical Foundation (Yamas & Niyamas):** Establish a strong moral and ethical groundwork (e.g., non-harming, truthfulness, self-restraint). A pure heart and disciplined conduct create a stable mind.

2. **Discipline the Body (Asana) and Breath (Pranayama):** Learn to hold a stable, comfortable posture. Master basic breath control techniques; they bridge body and mind, calming the nervous system.

3. **Master Concentration (Dharana):** Before attempting deep meditation, practice Dharana – the ability to fix your mind on a single point without distraction. This laser-like focus is foundational.

4. **Embrace Patience and Perseverance:** Progress is often subtle and non-linear. Cultivate immense patience and unwavering perseverance. Regularity in practice, even for short periods, is key.

5. **Seek Qualified Guidance:** Find a knowledgeable and compassionate teacher. Their wisdom and experience are invaluable in navigating the subtle inner terrain.

6. **Cultivate Sattva in Daily Life:** Consciously choose lifestyle practices that increase Sattva and reduce Rajas and Tamas, including wholesome food, positive company, and mindful engagement.

Mount of Ultimate Absorption (Mount Samadhi)

As I stood at the base of the towering Mountain of Samadhi, having just descended from the contemplative peaks of Dhyana, a stillness settled upon me. The air around felt different here—lighter, yet infinitely dense with unspoken potential. I closed my eyes, not in resignation, but in a deeper quest for inner vision. "How will I climb this mountain?" I wondered at the sheer scale of the endeavor, humbling me. "What landmarks will guide my ascent?" The questions echoed in the vastness before me, not demanding answers, but opening a space for inquiry. Just then, a gentle presence drew near. It was the enlightened yogi who had quietly accompanied my allegorical journey. With a serene smile, they acknowledged my unspoken queries. "This ascent," the yogi began, their voice a calming resonance, "is unlike any you have undertaken before. The landmarks here are not of stone and earth, but of consciousness itself. They are subtle shifts in perception, awakenings, and the gradual dissolution of all that is known." The yogi gestured towards the mountain, which, though still and imposing, now seemed to shimmer with an inner light. "We will begin by understanding that the path to Samadhi is less about scaling an external peak and more about dissolving the internal boundaries that obscure the summit. The 'climb' is a process of unlearning, of stripping away the layers that define our ordinary reality." With this initial guidance, the path ahead, while still mysterious, began to feel less daunting and more like an unfolding revelation.

The First Landmark: The Defined State

"Our very first step," the yogi elaborated, turning to face me fully, "is to truly grasp the nature of Samadhi itself, as the culmination of the preceding limbs. Recall Patanjali's precise definition from the *Yoga Sutras*."

तदेवार्थमात्रनिर्भासं स्वरूपशून्यमिव समाधिः ॥

(Tad evārthamātranirbhāsaṁ svarūpaśūnyam iva samādhiḥ)

"When the object of meditation alone shines forth, as if devoid of its own form, that is Samadhi."

"This sutra," the yogi continued, "describes the pinnacle of our journey through Dhārana and Dhyana. In Dhyana, we had a continuous flow of attention towards a single object. Here, in Samadhi, the mind's focus becomes so utterly absorbed that the meditator's own identity, or the 'form' of the thinking mind, seems to vanish. What remains is only the clear, unblemished light of the object of meditation. It is as if the lens through which we view reality has become perfectly transparent, leaving only the reality itself."

I pondered this shift. It wasn't about holding onto a thought, even a focused one, but rather, the merging of the observer and the observed. The 'landmark' wasn't a structure on the path, but the dissolution of the mental structure itself, allowing the essence of the chosen object—or perhaps, the essence of pure awareness-to shine without impediment. It felt less like an active striving and more like a sublime surrender, where the very act of knowing melted into pure being.

The Ultimate Merging: Echoes from Taittiriya

"This state, where the 'object alone shines forth'," the yogi continued, his gaze drifting towards the peak, "points towards the ultimate understanding that the Taittiriya Upanishad so eloquently describes. It speaks of the 'Self' or 'Atman' as being one with the 'Brahman,' the universal consciousness. This mountain's summit, ultimately, is not a place you arrive at externally, but a realization that blossoms internally: the indescribable merging of your individual consciousness with the larger, universal consciousness." I felt the resonance of this truth. The conceptual understanding of Samadhi, as the object shining forth, is now expanded to a more ineffable experience. It wasn't merely a refined state of attention, but an awareness of the very depth of one's being, transcending the boundaries of thought and language. The peak wasn't just a point of singular focus, but the dissolution of all perceived separateness, a return to an original, undivided reality that no mere words or thoughts could encapsulate. This understanding, whispered from ancient texts, transformed the mountain from a physical challenge into a spiritual revelation.

The Analogy of the Rivers to the Sea

"The sages of lore," the yogi then illuminated, "understood this ultimate merging through the timeless analogy of water. They described it as follows."

आकाशात्पतितं तोयं यथा गच्छति सागरम् ।

(Ākāśāt patitam toyam yathā gacchati sāgaram)

"As the water that falls from the sky (rain) coalesces into a stream, the stream carries the water ultimately to the sea, where it merges and becomes one with the vast expanse of the ocean."

He paused, letting the image settle. "This merging, where the individual drop of rain, having journeyed through stream and river, finally loses its distinct identity in the ocean, is the essence of the Advaita (non-dual) perspective on Samadhi. The self, as a separate entity, dissolves into the vast, undifferentiated ocean of Brahman. Yet," the yogi added, raising a finger, "the Dwaita (dualistic) perspective also offers a valuable insight: even as the drop merges, its constituent atoms, its essence, remain phenomenally part of the whole, a unique expression within the boundless unity. Both perspectives, in their own way, point to the incomprehensible transformation that occurs at the summit of this mountain."

Universal Echoes of the End State

"Indeed," the yogi affirmed, "this ultimate end-point, this liberation or union, resonates across the great mystical traditions of the world, though couched in their unique terminologies and metaphors. In Buddhism, the goal is Nirvana, the 'blowing out' of suffering, greed, hatred, and ignorance, leading to freedom from the cycle of rebirth (samsara)—a state beyond conditions, space, and time. For Sufi mystics in Islam, it is Fana (annihilation of the self) followed by Baqa (subsistence in God), where the individual ego dissolves into the Divine presence, yet a new, divinely-informed self remains, living in perfect harmony with God's will. In Christianity,

116

particularly in Eastern Orthodoxy, the concept of Theosis describes a transformative union with God, a 'deification' where humanity becomes like God, participating in the divine life without losing its created nature. The Beatific Vision in Western Christianity speaks of seeing God 'face to face' in heaven, experiencing ultimate happiness and direct knowledge of the Divine. Jewish mysticism, particularly Kabbalah, refers to Devekut, a clinging or cleaving to God, achieving intimacy and communion with the Divine, sometimes leading to the experience of *Olam Ha-Ba* (the World to Come) as a state of pure spiritual existence in God's presence. Even in Zoroastrianism, the concept of Frashokereti signifies a final renovation of the universe where evil is overcome, and all creation is restored to perfect unity and harmony with Ahura Mazda, indicating a collective spiritual perfection and integration."

The yogi's words painted a grand tapestry of human spiritual endeavor, each thread leading towards a similar, ineffable summit. It reinforced the idea that while our specific path is Yoga, the ultimate destination of liberation and union is a universal aspiration, understood and described through the lens of diverse traditions. This recognition broadened my sense of the mountain's significance, connecting my personal ascent to the collective spiritual quest of humanity.

The Surrealistic Ascent: Beyond Words and Sight

As the yogi finished speaking, the air around us seemed to thicken, not with humidity, but with an almost palpable mist of non-conceptual reality. The visual clarity of the mountain's features, which had previously served as conceptual markers, began to blur. My own senses, accustomed to defining and categorizing, found themselves increasingly inadequate. "From this point onward," the yogi's voice seemed to come from within me, echoing the fading external landscape, "our further travel will be almost surreal. A thick mist descends, concealing its reality from the grasp of ordinary words and sight. This is not a barrier, but an indication that the experience itself transcends the very tools we use to describe our waking world." I sensed the truth in his words. The vivid imagery of a physical climb, so useful for understanding the initial limbs of yoga, was now dissolving. The ascent was no longer about seeing a path or reaching a visible summit. Instead, it became an internal journey into a realm where the distinctions between 'self' and 'other,' 'here' and 'there,' 'words' and 'meaning' began to lose their hold. My eyes were open, yet what I saw was not of this world, and what I felt was beyond the capacity of language to capture. It was as if the very fabric of my perception was being gently, yet irrevocably, unwoven. The climb was no longer a physical exertion but a silent yielding to an incomprehensible transformation.

The AUM Manifestation: The Sonic Path to Turiya

"As the world around me became a blur of indistinct shapes, my awareness sharpened on the yogi's next guidance, which, though spoken, felt less like words and more like pure vibrational understanding. When words and sight fail to capture the states of consciousness, the ancient sages turned to sound – specifically, the primordial sound of AUM (Om) – as the ultimate descriptor and even the pathway. Each part of Om corresponds to a state of consciousness, leading us deeper towards the summit. Imagine this mountain," the yogi continued, his voice a resonant hum, "as a journey through the very dimensions of Om. We begin with 'A' (अ). This represents the Jagrat Avastha or the Waking State. It's the beginning of all experience, the state of outward consciousness where we perceive the physical world with our senses and intellect. It's the broad, expansive base of the mountain, where all phenomena are distinct and perceived. As we ascend, we move to 'U' (उ). This signifies the Svapna Avastha or the Dream State. (REM Sleep). Here, consciousness turns inward. We experience a world of subtle impressions, thoughts, and emotions, not bound by external reality. This is like moving higher on the mountain, where the physical landmarks become less defined, and our inner landscape of mind and subtle energies takes precedence. The objective world recedes, and the subjective, imaginative world unfolds. Further still, as we climb towards the heart of the mountain, we enter the silence of 'M' (म). This embodies the Sushupti Avastha or the Deep Sleep State. In this state, there are no dreams, no thoughts, no awareness of external objects. It's a state of peace and unified perception, a void from which all other states arise. This is like reaching a high plateau on the mountain, enveloped in a dense, peaceful mist where all form dissolves, and only undifferentiated consciousness remains, a deep reservoir of unmanifested potential. And then," the yogi's voice softened, almost becoming the silence itself, "at the very summit, beyond even the sound of 'M,' lies the Amātra – the Silence after AUM. This is the Turiya Avastha, the 'fourth state' of consciousness. It is the state of pure joy and peace, a

119

blissful silence that transcends all other states – waking, dreaming, or deep sleep. It is the ultimate fulfillment of life's purpose, the attainment of Bliss described as Satyam (Truth), Shivam (Goodness/Auspiciousness), Sundaram (Beauty). There is no sound here, no vibration, only the boundless, pure awareness. This is the Parama Shanti."

THE TEMPLE OF PRANAVA WHERE A SEEKER BECOMES A SIDDHA

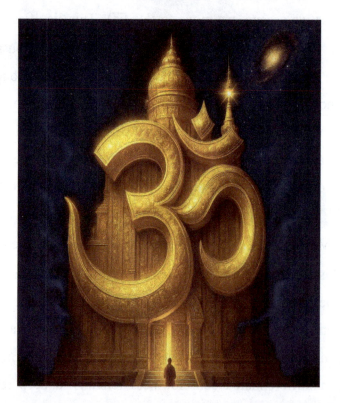

When the Prayer within the heart soars into an act of surrender, the sacred door opens to admit the seeker to the temple of ultimate reality, where he is liberated unto the land of pure JOY! Ultimate peace, where the individual consciousness fully realizes its non-duality with the universal, and the journey of Samadhi culminates in absolute liberation. "I closed my eyes, absorbing the truth of this sonic allegory. The Om symbol, once a simple sound, has now become a living map of consciousness itself, guiding me through its layers towards an unspeakable union. The silence after Om was not an absence, but a fullness, the true peak of the mountain where all seeking ceased in the embrace of pure, unconditioned bliss, The Ultimate Absorption: Brahmi State of Being."

"Indeed," the yogi affirmed, echoing my own sense of transcending mere categories. "At this stage of the ascent, the very concept of 'divisions' within Samadhi becomes largely academic. It is no longer about *achieving* a particular state, but about dissolving into the singular, ultimate reality. This is the voyage of absorption that leads to the ultimate Om state – the silence that embraces all sounds, the pure awareness that underlies all states of consciousness. This ultimate state of being, where individual consciousness merges completely with the Universal, is precisely what the Bhagavad Gita describes as Brāhmī Sthiti (ब्राह्मी स्थिति). In the second chapter, Krishna tells the following to Arjuna."

एषा ब्राह्मी स्थितिः पार्थ नैनां प्राप्य विमुह्यति । स्थित्वास्यामन्तकालेऽपि ब्रह्मनिर्वाणमृच्छति ॥

Eṣā brāhmī stitiḥ pārtha naināṁ prāpya vimuhyati / Sthitvāsyāmantakāle'pi brahmanirvāṇamṛcchati //

"This is the divine state, O son of Pritha, having attained which, one is never deluded. Being established in this state, even at the hour of death, one attains liberation in the domain of Brahman (Brahma-nirvana)."

The yogi's words resonated deeply. It was no longer about steps or types, but about *being*—a state of unwavering equilibrium and realization that transcended the temporal and the mundane. The mountain itself now felt less like an external climb and more like an inward unraveling, leading to this 'Brahmi Sthiti,' a state of abiding in the Divine, where the very purpose of existence found its blissful culmination. The mist of surreal reality had indeed become the veil of Maya, dissolving to reveal the ultimate truth.

The Summit Revealed: A Flood of Rapture and the Glimpse of Bimba Pratibimba

As the yogi spoke of the Brāhmī Sthiti, a flood of rapture or pure joy began to drown me. It wasn't an external sensation, but an overwhelming, internal effulgence, a sense of boundless peace and bliss that surged through every fiber of my being. The meticulous distinctions of Samadhi, the very concept of an ascent, all faded into insignificance in this rising tide of pure awareness.

Then came the crescendo, culminating in a crisis–not of distress, but of ultimate clarity. My eyes opened. There was no towering mountain, no guiding yogi, no intricate path. There was only I, sitting quietly, gazing at my familiar backyard pond. The elaborate allegory, the layers of philosophical discussion, had all dissolved. Yet, in that dissolution, a deeper reality manifested. I saw the sun's glimmering image reflected in the pond, dancing gently with the cool breeze. And in that simple reflection, the truth of Bimba (बिम्ब) and Pratibimba (प्रतिबिम्ब) struck me with the force of revelation. The Sun—that colossal, radiant source of energy, power, and light, sustaining all life on Earth—was the Bimba, the original. And its shimmering image in the pond, the Pratibimba, was the soul, the individual consciousness within all life. This 'Pratibimba' holds within it a tiny, precious fragment of the Bimba's will, its power, its light, yet with its own inherent limitations. It is this fragment that holds the potential to cleanse itself, to clarify its reflection, and ultimately, to realize its inherent unity with the boundless source.

This was the kernel of Yoga Shastra unveiled in a single, breathtaking moment: the understanding that the individual soul is a reflection of the Universal Self, and the journey of yoga is the purification of that reflection to realize oneness. A heartfelt gratitude welled up within me, a silent vow to dedicate my remaining life to all the good I could possibly do, grounded in this awakened truth. The search was over, not because the mountain was climbed, but because the mountain, and the climber, were realized as one with the pond, the sun, and everything in between.

An Epilogue; Conclusion

The dawn light filtered softly across the still waters of the hidden pond, its glassy surface a perfect reflection of the pastel sky. I found myself drawn to a smooth, moss-covered stone at the water's edge and settled there, surrounded by a riot of wildflowers and the pale blooms of lotus and water lilies drifting serenely. In that hushed morning air, my mind turned inward to the journey I had just completed, each mountain's lesson unfolding like a vivid tapestry, its wisdom etched indelibly into my heart.

I was acutely aware that the six peaks I had scaled and the formidable River of Pratyāhāra, I had crossed, still shimmered before my mind's eye, their contours stirring a deep, joyful remembrance. Yet the most extraordinary realization was that I had also ascended the final summit of Samādhi, not merely in metaphor, but as a tangible climb. The Yogi's luminous description of that ultimate encounter had been so vivid and compelling that I, too, felt the rough stone underfoot and sensed the radiant presence of ultimate reality unfolding at the summit.

I paused to marvel at why destiny, in its infinite grace, had bestowed upon me such an unexpected gift, a vivid, immersive vision, right on the very peak that embodied the true purpose of my entire yogic quest. Yet a question lingered in my heart: why? Why had the true ascent stepping foot upon that summit has been withheld from me?

As I lingered in Dhāraṇā, seeking clarity in the stillness, that inner silence was gently broken by a familiar voice. The very Yogi, serenity incarnate, who had guided my virtual ascent of Samādhi now sat beside me,

124

his countenance radiant and his tone suffused with benevolence. With an angelic smile and a voice as soft as dawn's first light, he met my gaze and said: "You are asking the question that all seekers, except a few advanced yoga practitioners, have asked over eons of time. Remember what Krishna gently told Arjuna in the Gītā-Yoga Śāstra."

मनुष्याणां सहस्रेषु कश्चिद्यतति सिद्धये ।
यततामपि सिद्धानां कश्चिन्मां वेत्ति तत्त्वतः ॥

manuṣyāṇāṃ sahasreṣu kaścin mayi yatati siddhyāya
yatatām api siddheṣu kaścin māṃ vetti tattvataḥ

"Among thousands of humans one may strive for perfection; among those who succeed, only one truly knows Me as I am. And after many lifetimes, the one of full knowledge finally surrenders unto Me."

"Among thousands of seekers who seek ultimate reality, only a few succeed. Among those who succeed only very few comprehend its true nature."

"He also affirmed that in the normal course of events attaining the ultimate enlightenment, it may take more than one birth."

बहूनां जन्मनामन्ते ज्ञानवान्मां प्रपद्यते ॥

bahūnāṃ janmanānte jñānavān māṃ prāpyate

"After multiple births of surviving fully enlightened you shall attain my domain."

"So your journey did not falter but reached its destined summit of enlightenment. Having absorbed the Yamas' code of conduct, embraced the Niyamas' inner disciplines, disciplined your body through Āsanas, mastered the breath in Prāṇāyāma, and transcended the senses at Pratyāhāra, fixed your mind in Dhāraṇā, dissolved into meditation in Dhyāna, and finally touched the boundless reality of Samādhi, you now return to Mother Earth. With the clarity of the summit still glowing within you and joined by kindred souls, you dedicate yourself— humble yet resolute, to address the

125

grave existential challenges gathering force around us, offering your wisdom and service, applying the transformative power of Yoga.

This, then, is the true meaning and purport of your journey—echoing the path of every yogic seeker who has come before you. In this age of Kali, we cannot rely on gods or angels to set things right as in mythic lore; the world's upheaval is of our own making, and only we can restore its balance. The ordered creation, once sustained by harmony and resilience, now runs wild in unmitigated chaos. Yet it is not too late—not to undo the past, but to delay the cycle of breakdown, to forestall the cataclysmic upheaval that resets creation, and to help usher in a new era founded on wisdom, compassion, and understanding. Meanwhile, each seeker emerges purified and illumined by this inner odyssey, carrying a spark of yogic wisdom into the world. United by that flame, you become part of a critical multitude men and women empowered to confront the existential crises threatening human progress. Let us invoke, together, the timeless benediction of ancient wisdom."

ॐ सह नाववतु।
सह नौ भुनक्तु।
सह वीर्यं करवावहै।
तेजस्वि नावधीतमस्तु मा विद्विषावहै॥

oṃ saha nāvavatu |
saha nau bhunaktu |
saha vīryaṃ karavāvahai |
tejasvi nāvadhītamastu mā vidviṣāvahai ||

"May we be protected together, may we be nourished together, may we work together with great vigor, may our study be illuminating, and may we not hate one another."

Reverie: The Meadow of Reflections

As we lingered at the foothills, seven of us remained—five seasoned in age and two much younger, a thoughtful man and his serene female companion. Though the journey of seven ascents and the perilous crossing was complete, our hearts were reluctant to return home. Drawn by the beauty of that paradise, with its ponds and flowered paths, we wandered along a quiet trail that curved gently into a hidden valley.

The air was hushed, as if nature itself had paused in reverence. Soon the path opened into a clearing of extraordinary beauty—a broad meadow carpeted in soft grass, bordered by tall, whispering trees. At its heart lay a crystal pool, still as glass, mirroring the sky above.

To our astonishment, there we found awaiting us the venerable guides of our last ascents—a Yogi and a Yogini, radiant in their simplicity, ageless in their wisdom, appearing fitter than their years. We approached with reverence, sensing that this meeting was no chance occurrence but a gift bestowed at the culmination of our pilgrimage.

They greeted us with serene smiles and invited us to sit by the water's edge. The pond, they said, was no ordinary pool but a mirror of the soul, where each traveler might see not the outer visage but the inner record of the journey. One by one, we gazed into its depths and beheld our struggles, faltering steps, unexpected courage, and quiet triumphs that had brought us to this sacred moment.

It was then that the younger man stepped forward. His voice trembled slightly, for he carried not only his own questions but also the burdens of a restless age. With a respectful bow, he asked, **"How does the path of yoga, as we have lived it in this vision, help us face the strains of modern life— the unrelenting stress, the digital noise, the ceaseless distractions?"**

The Yogi's eyes softened as he looked upon him. His reply came slowly and gently, like a stream flowing over polished stones. "Stress is the cry of imbalance within, and the limbs of yoga restore balance step by step. The Yamas and Niyamas form the foundation of clarity and restraint. Asanas strengthen and steady the body, the abode of the soul. Pranayama calms the currents of breath and mind. Dharana trains the attention so that one is no longer enslaved by distractions. And in Dhyana, the mind finds its own vast stillness where peace blooms. What modern science calls stress management, yoga knows as harmony of being, cultivated patiently until no storm from without can disturb the calm within."

The young man's eyes brightened as he listened, and many of us nodded in agreement, for we had tasted this truth upon our own climbs.

Encouraged by the depth of this answer, the young woman now lifted her voice. With quiet earnestness, she asked, **"But what of the wider world? Our societies are torn by ecological ruin, by inequality, by disconnection. Is yoga merely a refuge for the self, or does it also speak to these greater wounds?"**

The Yogini responded with a voice calm and luminous, her words carrying the quiet force of conviction. "Yoga is never for the self alone. The one who climbs these mountains returns not empty-handed but transformed and empowered. Compassion ripens, and responsibility awakens. The oneness felt in meditation naturally extends to all living beings. Such awareness tempers greed, guides consumption, inspires service. Thus, ecological care, social healing, and unity arise not as imposed duties but as natural fruits of vision. When enough hearts are illumined in this way, society itself bends toward wholeness."

A hush fell among us as she spoke, and we felt these were not lofty ideals but living truths already embodied in her presence.

For a long moment, we sat in silence. Then one of the older pilgrims, seasoned in years and tempered by long experience, leaned forward. His voice carried both gravity and unease as he asked, **"Science races ahead, machines now imitate thought, and humanity seems unsure of its path. What role has yoga yet to play?"**

The Yogi and Yogini turned to one another, and then, as if with one breath, their voices rose together—calm and resonant, like twin streams joining into a single river. "Science unveils the outer workings of the universe, but yoga unveils the inner essence of being. The world to come will need both. Without wisdom, technology becomes a runaway chariot. Without compassion, knowledge becomes a tool of exploitation. Yoga anchors progress in conscience, teaching that true advancement is measured not by power but by harmony—between body and spirit, humanity and nature, the finite and the infinite. This is the hope for your century: not the rejection of modernity but its guidance by the eternal light within."

The elder bowed his head slowly, as if in solemn recognition, while the younger seekers watched him with newfound respect. Their doubts softened into quiet resolve. And we all felt the same—that these answers were not for him alone but for every seeker of our age.

We lingered long in that meadow, embraced by silence and light, realizing that our pilgrimage was not ending but beginning anew. The return to the world was as sacred as the climb itself. And the meadow, with its pond of reflections, would remain within us as an inner sanctuary wherever life's journey might lead.

Then, as though offering a blessing for the road ahead, the Yogi and Yogini spoke once more. "O returning pilgrims, our heartfelt wishes go with you for the success of the challenges that await. Remember this: when the pilgrims of this planet, its leaders and its stewards, grow together and reach the critical number required, a great restoration of faith and righteousness will begin. Then the evil forces corroding what some of you call the Anthropocene may at last be confronted, slowed, and, if the laws of karma allow, even reversed. Yet do not burden yourselves with fear of outcomes. The true prize lies in the process itself. Walk your path with courage, with compassion, with truth. Safe return, and Godspeed in your mission. We shall be with you always, unseen but near, ready to guide when you call."

With that, they raised their hands in a gesture of benevolent goodwill. With folded hands, we bowed in gratitude, bidding them farewell, and began our journey home.

Yoga Beyond the Mat (A Guide for Our Time and All Generations)

As we close this visionary journey across the mountains of the Eightfold Path, a final question lingers in the heart of the reader: "Can I truly live this path here, now, in my own world?" The answer is clear, enduring, and compassionate:

Yes, you can. Not only can you, you must.

Yoga was never meant to be confined to Himalayan caves or spiritual retreats. It was born in life, for life. It is for the mother balancing work and family, the executive pacing through deadlines, the elder seeking grace, the student hungering for purpose. It is for those facing grief and for those in love with living. Yoga is for **you**, exactly where you are, exactly as you are.

This chapter is not an ending, but a new beginning—a living guide for embracing yoga amid the complexity and beauty of modern life. May it serve as your trusted companion and steadfast compass, pointing you toward balance, clarity, and inner peace each day.

Chair Yoga: For the Elderly, the Disabled, and the Desk-Bound

Yoga does not demand acrobatic feats or perfect posture. It meets the practitioner where they are, with grace and gentleness. Chair yoga is ideal for those with physical limitations: the elderly, those recovering from illness, or anyone seated for long hours. With simple stretches, mindful breathing, and seated Pranayama, one can nourish joints, release tension, and cultivate inner balance. The body you have today is the perfect starting place.

Sleep Yoga: For the Restless and Anxious

In a world of overstimulation, insomnia and mental fatigue have become commonplace. Yoga Nidra, the yogic sleep, is a method of guided relaxation that brings profound rest to the body while maintaining subtle awareness. It resets the nervous system, dissolves anxiety, and restores peace, helping you fall asleep not out of exhaustion, but through surrender.

Yoga for the Super-Busy Executive

Success today often comes at the cost of health, relationships, and peace of mind. Yet, the most effective leaders are not those who are frantic, but those who are centered. Even the busiest executive can reclaim composure through micro-practices: deep breaths before meetings, five rounds of Surya Namaskar at dawn, mindful meals, and reflective journaling. These brief practices sharpen decision-making and diffuse stress, without requiring escape from the boardroom.

Yoga for Students and Aspirants

For students and young professionals, yoga is not a luxury; it is a necessity. In a hypercompetitive world, yoga cultivates clarity of thought, emotional regulation, and the ability to focus without burnout.

Breathwork before study, posture during breaks, and stillness at night form a triad that strengthens not just the brain but the mind.

Yoga for Caregivers and Homemakers

Those who care for others — parents, homemakers, nurses, and teachers, often neglect themselves. Yoga reminds them: to serve well, you must first be whole. Ten minutes of stillness, conscious breath while completing chores, and weekly self-care rituals can restore depleted energies and rekindle joy. Yoga is not selfish; it is **self-sustaining**.

Yoga in Times of Grief, Pain, and Recovery

In moments of loss or fragility, words may fail, but breath does not. Gentle movement, mantra, and silent sitting become sacred allies. Yoga does not promise to remove sorrow. But it offers a compassionate way to **hold it**, to breathe through it, and to heal with time.

Yoga on the Move

Travel, transition, and unpredictability often disrupt wellness routines. Yet yoga travels lightly. A breath practice on a plane, mindful walking in a hotel corridor, or simply grounding your feet during a busy day, these are enough to stay anchored. True yogis are not identified by their setting, but by their stillness **within**.

A Golden Hour: A Daily Life Strategy

If you can offer your day just **one golden hour** — divided in moments if needed, it will return to you in richness.

- 20 minutes of breath and movement in the morning
- 10 minutes of mindfulness during the day

- 20 minutes of reflection or silence in the evening
- 10 minutes of peace before sleep

In just one hour a day, a different kind of life unfolds, **balanced, grounded, and deeply alive.**

Yoga as an Antidote to the Deadly Stress of Modern Living

Today's world exerts pressure on every front: economic, social, and psychological. Stress is no longer occasional; it is endemic. Yet, it is not inevitable.

Yoga is a systemic antidote. It lowers cortisol, rewires the nervous system, and shifts perception from survival to serenity. And when practiced not just individually, but collectively, yoga becomes a **cultural force.**

In classrooms, it teaches focus and kindness. In hospitals, it heals more than the body. In politics, it brings conscience to policy. In economics, it tempers greed with sufficiency. And in development, it reminds us that **progress is not only material, but ethical and spiritual.**

Yoga, lived sincerely, not only changes lives **it can change the world.**

Yoga Is Not Just for the Next Life — It's for This One

Some believe yoga is about preparing for a better next birth. But yoga is not postponement. It is present. Yoga is for now, for this life, for this breath. It doesn't demand you abandon joy, it teaches you how to savor it **without clinging**. You can have your cake and enjoy the icing too, if you eat it with attention, gratitude, and grace. Yoga is not repression. It is intelligent enjoyment, guided by inner stillness. It is not a denial of life, **it is the art of living it well.**

Final Reflection: You Are Already on the Path

You have read this book. You have walked the mountain trails in your mind. You have paused by rivers, touched the clouds of subtle truths, and gazed inward into the temple of silence. If something in you has awakened, even slightly, you are already on the path.

Let yoga walk beside you through the joys and challenges of your daily life. Let it nourish you, refine you, strengthen you. Let it help you grow not away from the world, **but deeper into it with wisdom, compassion, and equanimity.** You do not need to change your life, only how you **live** it. You are not too late. You are not too burdened. You are not unqualified. You are already on the path. Now... just keep walking.

A Closing Note of Gratitude and Blessing

To all readers, seekers, and fellow travelers: This book has been the offering of a lifetime spent in medicine, in service, and in spiritual reflection. It is born of lived experience, of practicing yoga not in the shelter of monasteries, but amid the duties of professional life, international work, and family care.

If this vision has stirred a thought, softened a feeling, or lit a flame within you, then its purpose is fulfilled. I leave you with a blessing, ancient in origin but universal in spirit, expressed herein in English for all to receive fully:

May all beings be happy. May all be free from illness. May all see only what is noble and uplifting. May none suffer in any way. May peace prevail, in body, in mind, and in spirit.

With gratitude and goodwill,

— Gururaj Mutalik, MD

Bibliography and Recommended Reading

1. Aranya, H. (1981). *Yoga Philosophy of Patanjali* (P. N. Mukerji, Trans.). SUNY Press.

2. Aurobindo, S. (1999). *The Integral Yoga: Sri Aurobindo's Teaching and Method of Practice.* Lotus Press.

3. Bihar School of Yoga, 19 Mallinson, James, trans. *Gheranda Samhita.* YogaVidya.com, 2004.

4. Bryant, E. F. (2009). *The Yoga Sutras of Patañjali: A New Edition, Translation, and Commentary.* North Point Press.

5. Desikachar, T. K. V. (1995). *The Heart of Yoga: Developing a Personal Practice.* Inner Traditions.

6. Easwaran, E. (2007). *The Bhagavad Gita* (2nd ed.). Nilgiri Press.

7. Eliade, M. (1958). *Yoga: Immortality and Freedom.* Princeton University Press.

8. Goldsmith, J. S. (1991). *The Art of Meditation.* Harper & Row.

9. James Haughton Woods. *The Yoga-System of Patanjali.* M.B. Publishers, 1971.

10. Jois, K. P. (1999). *Yoga Mala.* North Point Press.

11. Kriyananda, S. (2010). *The Essence of the Bhagavad Gita: Explained by Paramhansa Yogananda.* Crystal Clarity Publishers.

12. Kriyananda, Swami. *The Essence of the Bhagavad Gita: Explained by Paramhansa Yogananda.* Crystal Clarity Publishers, 2008.

13. Mallinson, J. (Trans.). (2004). *Gheranda Samhita.* YogaVidya.com.

14. Prabhavananda, S., & Isherwood, C. (1953). *How to Know God: The Yoga Aphorisms of Patanjali*. Vedanta Press.

15. Prabhavananda, Swami, and Christopher Isherwood. *How to Know God: The Yoga Aphorisms of Patanjali*.

16. Prof. K.T. Pandurangi. *Essentials of Upanishads*. Poorna Prajna Vidyapeetha Banglor, 1991.

17. Prof. K.T. Pandurangi. *The Principal Upanishads*. Dvaita Vedanta Studies and Research Foundation, 1999.

18. Radhanath Swami. (2010). *The Journey Home: Autobiography of an American Swami*. Mandala Publishing.

19. Rama, S. (1986). *Path of Fire and Light: Advanced Practices of Yoga*. Himalayan Institute Press.

20. Rama, S. (1998). *Living with the Himalayan Masters*. Himalayan Institute Press.

21. Rama, Swami. *Living with the Himalayan Masters*. Himalayan Institute Press, 1998.

22. Rama, Swami. *Path of Fire and Light: Advanced Practices of Yoga*. Himalayan Institute Press, 1986.

23. Satchidananda, S. (1978). *The Yoga Sutras of Patanjali: Commentary by Sri Swami Satchidananda*. Integral Yoga Easwaran, Eknath. *The Bhagavad Gita*. 2nd ed., Nilgiri Press, 2007.

24. Sivananda, S. (1994). *The Science of Pranayama*. The Divine Life Society.

25. Sri Aurobindo. *The Synthesis of Yoga*. Lotus Press, 1996.

26. Swatmarama, S. (1985). *Hatha Yoga Pradipika* (Swami Muktibodhananda, Trans.). Bihar School of Yoga.

27. Swatmarama, Swami. *Hatha Yoga Pradipika.* Translated by Herder and Herder, Inc . The Aquarian Press 1992.

28. Veda Iyengar, B. K. S. *Light on Yoga.* Schocken Books, 1966.

29. Vivekananda, S. (1896/2001). *Raja Yoga.* Advaita Ashrama.

30. Yogananda, P. (1946). *Autobiography of a Yogi.* Self-Realization Fellowship.

References of source books for readers

1. Alter, Joseph S. 2004. *Yoga in Modern India: The Body between Science and Philosophy*. Princeton, NJ: Princeton University Press.

2. Baird, Amy L. 2014. *Rediscovering Shakti: The Power of the Feminine Path*. Rochester, VT: Inner Traditions.

3. Bryant, Edwin F., ed. 2009. *The Yoga Sūtras of Patañjali: A New Edition, Translation, and Commentary*. New York: North Point Press.

4. Burley, Mikel. 2000. "Hinduism, Yoga, and the Therapeutic: Aspirations, Practices, and Outcomes." *Journal of Alternative and Complementary Medicine* 6 (2): 149–57.

5. Büssing, Arndt, Klaus Ostermann, and Michael Büssing. 2012. "Effects of Yoga Interventions on Pain and Pain-Associated Disability: A Meta-Analysis." *Journal of Pain* 13 (1): 1–9.

6. Chowdhury, Gautam. 2013. "Yoga as a Tool for Stress Management in the Workplace." *Occupational Medicine* 63 (7): 465–68.

7. Cramer, Holger, Michael Haller, Gustav Lauche, Gustav Dobos, and Andreas Michalsen. 2016. "A Systematic Review and Meta-Analysis of Yoga for Low Back Pain." *Clinical Journal of Pain* 32 (10): 800–16.

8. Damodaran, Malathi, Satya Murthy, and S. Patil. 2002. "Therapeutic Role of Yoga in Type 2 Diabetes." *Journal of the Association of Physicians of India* 50 (5): 633–36.

9. De Michelis, Elizabeth, ed. 2005. *Contemporary Yoga: Innovation and Tradition*. London: Continuum.

10. De Michelis, Elizabeth. 2004. *A History of Modern Yoga: Patanjali and Western Esotericism*. London: Continuum.

11. Devananda, Shiva Rea. 2002. *Kundalini Yoga: The Flow of Eternal Power*. Garden City, NY: Anchor.

12. Feuerstein, Georg. 1998. *The Yoga Tradition: Its History, Literature, Philosophy and Practice*. Prescott, AZ: Hohm Press.

13. Feuerstein, Georg. 2002. *The Deeper Dimension of Yoga: Theory and Practice*. Boston: Shambhala.

14. Feuerstein, Georg. 2008. "The Origins and History of Hatha Yoga." *The Journal of Transpersonal Psychology* 40 (2): 89–104.

15. Fishbein, Diana P., and Anita K. Dolan. 2010. "Yoga and Quality of Life: A Review." *Journal of Psychiatric Practice* 16 (2): 95–105.

16. Fishbein, Diana. 2002. "Yoga in Public Schools: A Content Analysis of the Literature." *Yoga Journal* 20 (4): 42–49.

17. Fishbein, Diana. 2010. "Yoga in American Hospitals: A Survey of Hospital Programs." *Journal of Holistic Nursing* 28 (3): 207–17.

18. Futrell, Malcolm D. 2009. *Naked Seeing: The Great Perception Sutra*. New York: Columbia University Press.

19. Gard, Tim. 2013. "Feasibility of an Online Yoga Program for Stress Management." *Complementary Therapies in Clinical*

Practice 19 (3): 150–56.

20. Gyawali, Gorky. 2015. "Yoga and Mental Health: A Meta-Review." *International Journal of Yoga Therapy* 25 (1): 37–44.

21. *Haṭha Yoga Pradīpikā*. 2000. Translated by James Mallinson and Mark Singleton. Oxford: Oxford University Press.

22. Iyengar, Geeta S. 2005. *Yoga: A Gem for Women*. Boston: Shambhala.

23. Jain, Andrea R., and Michelle T. King, eds. 2010. *Beyond Enlightenment: Buddhism, Religion, Modernity*. Albany: SUNY Press.

24. Jain, Andrea. 2014. *Selling Yoga: From Counterculture to Pop Culture*. Oxford: Oxford University Press.

25. James Haughton Woods. "The Yoga-System of Patanjali". M.B. Publishers, 1971. 62. IIT Kanpur. *The Geeta supersite.* *https://www.gitasupersite.iitk.ac.in/*

26. Khalsa, Sat Bir S. 2004. "Yoga as a Clinical Intervention: A Bibliometric Analysis." *Journal of Alternative and Complementary Medicine* 10 (2): 251–56.

27. Mallinson, James, and Mark Singleton. 2017. *Roots of Yoga*. London: Penguin Classics.

28. McCall, Timothy. 2007. *The Yoga of Breath: A Step-by-Step Guide to Prāṇāyāma*. Boston: Shambhala.

29. McCall, Timothy. 2013. *Yoga as Medicine: The Yogic Prescription for Health and Healing*. New York: Bantam.

30. Müller-Ebeling, Christian, Bettina, and Wolf-Dietrich. 2011.

Yoga and Ayurveda: Self-Healing and Self-Realization. Twin
Lakes, WI: Lotus Press.

31. Pandurangi, K. T. 1986. *Shatprasna, Atharvana, and Mandukya
Upanisads: With Madhvacharya's Bhasya.* Bengaluru: Dvaita
Vedanta Studies and Research Foundation.

32. Pandurangi, K. T. 1999. *The Principal Upanisads: With Notes
According to Madhvacharya's Bhasya.* Vol. 1. Bengaluru:
Dvaita Vedanta Studies and Research Foundation.

33. Pandurangi, K. T. 2006. *Essentials of Tatparya Chandrika and
Sloka Tatparya Chandrika of Sri Vyasatirtha.* USA: World
Forum of Sri Vyasaraja Devotees.

34. Pandurangi, K. T. 2010. *Essentials of Upanisads: According to
Sri Madhvacharya's Bhasya.* Bengaluru: Dvaita Vedanta Studies
and Research Foundation.

35. Pandurangi, K. T. 2014. *The Principal Upanisads.* Vols. 1–2.
Bengaluru: Dvaita Vedanta Studies and Research Foundation.

36. Patanjali. 2009. *The Yoga Sūtras of Patañjali.* 2nd ed. Translated
by Edwin F. Bryant. New York: North Point Press.

37. Peng, Clement, Annabelle Tung, and Hema Subramanian. 2011.
"Yoga for Cardiovascular Risk Reduction." *American Journal of
Cardiology* 108 (5): 726–28.

38. Radhakrishnan, Sarvepalli, and Charles A. Moore, eds. 1957. *A
Sourcebook in Indian Philosophy.* Princeton, NJ: Princeton
University Press.

39. Ross, Aileen, and Antoinette Thomas. 2010. "The Health

Benefits of Yoga and Exercise: A Review of Comparison Studies." *Journal of Alternative and Complementary Medicine* 16 (1): 3–12.

40. Śaṅkara. 2003. *Commentary on the Yoga Sūtras*. Translated by Chip Hartranft. Albany: State University of New York Press.

41. Saraswati, Swami Satyananda. 2001. *Four Chapters on Freedom: Commentary on the Yoga Sūtras of Patañjali*. Munger, India: Yoga Publications Trust.

42. Saraswati, Swami Sivananda. 1987. *The Science of Prāṇāyāma*. Munger, India: Yoga Publications Trust.

43. Sharma, B. N. Krishnamurti. 1961. *Dvaita Philosophy as Expounded by Śrī Madhvācārya*. Chennai: University of Madras.

44. Sharma, B. N. Krishnamurti. 1983. *Madhva's Aupaniṣadam Darśanam*. Bengaluru: Dvaita Vedanta Studies and Research Foundation.

45. Sharma, B. N. Krishnamurti. 2008. *History of the Dvaita School of Vedānta and Its Literature: From the Earliest Beginnings to Our Own Times*. 3rd ed. New Delhi: Motilal Banarsidass.

46. Sharma, B. N. Krishnamurti. 2008. *The Brahmasūtras and Their Principal Commentaries: A Critical Exposition*. Vols. I–III. New Delhi: Munshiram Manoharlal Publishers.

47. Sherman, Keith, and Thomas R. E. Barnes. 2015. "Review of *Roots of Yoga*, by James Mallinson and Mark Singleton." *Journal of the American Academy of Religion* 83 (2): 584–87.

48. Singleton, Mark, and Ellen Goldberg. 2014. "Northern

Kentucky's Yoga Craze and Postural Orthodoxy." *Journal of Yoga Studies* 7 (1): 23–44.

49. Singleton, Mark. 2008. "Between the Esoteric and the Apparatus: Hatha Yoga and the Colonial Encounter." *South Asia Research* 28 (2): 153–70.

50. Singleton, Mark. 2010. *Yoga Body: The Origins of Modern Posture Practice*. Oxford: Oxford University Press.

51. Sri Aurobindo. "The Synthesis of Yoga". Lotus Press, 1996.

52. Strauss, Sarah. 2005. *Positioning Yoga: Balancing Acts across Cultures*. London: Berg.

53. Telles, Shirley, Sat Bir S. Khalsa, and Paul M. Balkrishna. 2012. "Yoga as a Therapeutic Intervention: A Bibliometric Analysis of Published Research Studies." *Indian Journal of Physiology and Pharmacology* 56 (1): 8–13.

54. Timmons, Brooke W., Jennifer Nordin, and Catherine M. Cairney. 2012. "Physical Activity and School Performance." *Pediatric Exercise Science* 24 (1): 110–19.

55. Veda Iyengar, B. K. S. 1966. *Light on Yoga: Yoga Dipika*. London: George Allen & Unwin.

56. Vivekananda, Swami. 1896. *Raja Yoga*. Madras: The Ramakrishna Vivekananda Center.

57. Wei, Faming, Eun-Kyoung O, Veda M. Johnson, and Raghuveer M. Chary. 2014. "Effects of Yoga on Oxidative Stress and DNA Damage in Healthy Volunteers." *Journal of Complementary and Integrative Medicine* 11 (2): 121–27.

58. White, David Gordon. 2012. *The Yoga Sutra of Patanjali: A Biography*. Princeton, NJ: Princeton University Press.

59. White, David Gordon. 2014. "Unbroken Continuity? The Myth of Yoga's Transmission." *Journal of Yoga Studies* 9 (1): 12–29.

60. *Yoga Vedanta Forest Academy Lectures*. 2002. Sivananda Forest, Munger, India: Yoga Publications Trust.

The Voice of Humanity

(Timeless Wisdom of Thought Leaders of Humanity)

1. Invocation

Let noble thoughts come to us from every side. — **Rigveda** We gather as one human family, seekers across centuries, to declare the wisdom of all who have walked before us. In every language and symbol, a single voice speaks — calling us to truth, compassion, and unity.

2. Ancient Wisdom Across Cultures

- **Hindu (Upanishads)**: *To the Righteous and the Enlightened, the entire universe is our family,*

- **Buddhist (Dhammapada)**: "Hatred does not cease by hatred, but only by love."

- **Christian (Sermon on the Mount)**:

    - "Blessed are the peacemakers, for they shall be called children of God." "Love your enemies and pray for those who persecute you."

      "Whatever you wish that others would do to you, do also to them."

    - **Jewish (Torah)**: "Justice, justice shall you pursue." — *Deuteronomy 16:20*

    - **Islamic (Prophet Muhammad, Hadith)**: "The best among you are those who bring benefit to others."

    - **Sufi (Rumi)**: "You are not a drop in the ocean. You are the entire ocean in a drop."

    - **Taoist (Lao Tzu)**: "To understand others is knowledge. To understand yourself is wisdom."

    - **Confucian (Analects)**: "The strength of a nation derives from the integrity of the home."

- **Zoroastrian**: "Good thoughts, good words, good deeds."
- **Indigenous (Various)**: "We do not inherit the Earth from our ancestors; we borrow it from our children."
- **African (Ubuntu)**: "I am because we are."
- **Ancient Greek (Delphi)**: "Know thyself."

3. Philosophers and Reformers

- **Plato**: "Knowledge which is acquired under compulsion obtains no hold on the mind."
- **Socrates**: "The unexamined life is not worth living."
- **Confucius**: "Do not impose on others what you do not wish for yourself."
- **Rousseau**: "Man is born free, and everywhere he is in chains."
- **Mary Wollstonecraft**: "I do not wish women to have power over men, but over themselves."
- **Mahatma Gandhi**: "Be the change you wish to see in the world."
- **Martin Luther King Jr.**: "Injustice anywhere is a threat to justice everywhere."

4. The Voice of Science and Wonder

- **Galileo Galilei**: "And yet it moves." — Truth remains, even when denied.
- **Isaac Newton**: Revealed harmony in motion, uniting heaven and earth through natural law.
- **Charles Darwin**: "There is grandeur in this view of life…" — All life is part of one evolving web.
- **Albert Einstein**: "The most beautiful thing we can experience is the mysterious."

- **Erwin Schrödinger**: "The total number of minds in the universe is one." — A vision of unified consciousness.
- **Richard Feynman**: "I... a universe of atoms, an atom in the universe." — Wonder as the language of science.
- **Carl Sagan**: "We are made of star stuff." — The cosmos knows itself through us.
- **Rachel Carson**: "In nature, nothing exists alone." — We live in ecological interdependence.
- **Jane Goodall**: "What you do makes a difference." — Compassion is itself a science of connection.
- **Stephen Hawking**: "Look up at the stars and not down at your feet." — Our gaze defines our destiny.
- **Yuval Noah Harari**: "We are now gods — but for lack of wisdom." — Knowledge demands responsibility.

5. Contemporary Reflections

- Our planet warms, seas rise, species vanish—may conscience awaken.
- Digital networks bind us—let them not fracture our humanity.
- Power concentrates—may justice keep pace.
- We possess more knowledge than ever—let humility guide its use.

Closing Invocation — Rabindranath Tagore, Gitanjali 35

Where the mind is without fear and the head is held high; Where knowledge is free; Where the world has not been broken up into fragments by narrow domestic walls; Where words come out from the depth of truth; Where tireless striving stretches its arms towards perfection; Where the clear stream of reason has not lost its way into the dreary desert sand of dead habit; Where the mind is led forward by thee into ever-widening thought and action— Into that heaven of freedom, my Father, let my country awake.

Our Next Book: THE OM WAY

A New Vision for Humanity

Our Next book on "The Chaos of the Anthropocene to the Harmony of the Omcene"

Gururaj Mutalik and Bhushan Patwardhan

What lies beyond the Anthropocene, an age marked by dominance, disconnection, and ecological distress? *The Om Way* offers a considered and deeply human response, born from the confluence of two life journeys across different generations. Written by Dr. Gururaj Mutalik, a ninety-seven-year-old physician scientist and global health leader, and Professor Bhushan Patwardhan, a sixty-five-year-old biochemist and integrative health researcher, this book charts a path from distraction to stillness, from scattered information to coherent wisdom, from imbalance to harmony. The narrative begins with Dr. Mutalik's own lived experience of walking *The Om Way,* reversing serious metabolic dysfunction in his nineties and regaining vitality through the integration of modern medicine, Ayurveda, Yoga, and disciplined lifestyle changes. From this deeply personal starting point, the book expands into a reflection on the state of our planet, our societies, and our inner lives. It introduces the concept of the Omcene, both a horizon for humanity and a transformation in consciousness, and rests on two central frameworks. The first is the Six Evils (6Es): Desire, Anger, Greed, Delusion, Pride, and Envy, enduring inner forces that fuel unrest. The second is the Six Dangers of Modern Aging (6Ds): Diabetes, Dementia, Depression, Disability, Dependence, and Death, outward expressions of imbalance in contemporary societies. The book then charts Six Milestones (6Ms) as steps toward a more balanced and harmonious way of living. At the heart of *The Om Way* is *pratyahara*, the art of turning the senses inward to reclaim mental space, clarity, and freedom from compulsive reaction. Through personal stories, philosophical insight, and evidence from science and tradition, this book invites readers into a reflective yet practical journey from the turbulence of the Anthropocene to the harmony of the Omcene. It honors rigorous science while embracing lived truth, intuitive insight, and the deeper dimensions of human experience.

Vision

We acknowledge the Anthropocene as a time of imbalance, ecological, social, and personal, and present *The Om Way* as a path to rebalancing both within and without. The Omcene is described not only as a possible future era but as a shift in consciousness: from fragmentation to coherence, from domination to reverence, from exploitation to compassion, from ego to humility, from knowledge to wisdom, and from awareness to a deeper, unifying consciousness. This transformation can be understood as a progression: from ignorance to knowledge, from knowledge to integrated understanding, and from there to wisdom that shapes how we live, age, and meet the end of life. It is the timeless movement from darkness to light, from fear to trust, from the weight of mortality to the hope of inner freedom.

Meaning and purpose are central to this shift. Civilizations are not renewed by technology or control alone. Ancient, time-tested wisdom and modern science must work together so that knowledge serves life and collective well-being. Pratyahara offers a practical entry into this rebalancing by quieting sensory overload and cultivating steadiness, discernment, and selfmastery. The compass of the Omcene is universal. It resonates with the spirit that *the world is one family* and *may all be free from illness*. It calls for a culture that chooses harmony over chaos, significance over metrics, depth over haste, connection over consumption, sufficiency over excess, and compassion over hatred.

This book is now in the final stages of completion, and it is fair to expect its appearance on bookshelves within the next two months.

Acknowledgements

The journey of preparing this labor of love would not have reached completion without the support, assistance, and inspiration of many. I offer my deepest gratitude to the following individuals:

To my dear daughter, **Madhuri**, for her loving care along with **Ujjal Mukherjee** who generously made it possible for me to be gently settled into my new "yogic home" in Montclair, close to where they live. Madhuri also gave thoughtful advice on many important matters related to this book. Her son, **Sanjay**, is helping share its message through social media, while my grandson, **Roy Mutalik**, has supported me with video editing and my YouTube channel.

I am equally grateful to my son **Madhav** and his wife **Sujata**, who have supported me in countless ways through all my efforts. I am also thankful to my eldest son, **Pradeep**, and his wife **Meenakshi**, who cared for me when I was unwell. My youngest son, **Praveen**, and his gracious wife **Karen**, have inspired me with his photography, flower breeding, and deep love for animals.

A special thank you goes to my grandnephew **Vaibhav Katti**, whose tireless help and deep knowledge of computer technology—especially artificial intelligence—allowed me to use multiple AI platforms for research, editing, and the creation of beautiful images.

I also thank my grandnephew **Sameer Mahuli** for building my website, assisting me during my India visits, and helping in many other ways.

My heartfelt thanks to my dear friend **Anil Deshpande**, a kind and generous person whose guidance and practical help supported me throughout. I am also grateful to **Vaibhav Joshi**, a dedicated yoga practitioner and accomplished professional, for his valuable assistance. I deeply appreciate **Mr. Brahm Agarwal**, an entrepreneur and supporter of ancient traditions, for his encouragement and support.

I thank my physicians, especially **Dr. Saurabh Choksi**, for his caring advice and help in maintaining my health. He is gifted in both modern cardiology and traditional healing and brings to his work the heart of a seeker, artist, poet, and music lover. I also thank **Dr. Hoshidar Tamboli**, a cardiologist with a sincere interest in yoga and meditation, for his generous support of this project.

Warm thanks to my extended medical family, especially my former students at **B.J. Medical College**, who have graciously acknowledged my contributions through their digital platform, *BJMedicine*. Their continued camaraderie has meant a great deal to me.

I fondly remember many among them: **Dr. Shashi Sangle**, **Dr. Ravi Gulati**, **Dr. Subhas Kale**, **Dr. Chittranjan Yajnik**, **Dr. Sudhir Kothari**, **Dr. Erach Bharucha** and his wife **Kapila**, **Dr. Nasli Ichaporia**, **Dr. Rajani Amin**, **Dr. Milind Phadke**, and **Dr. Vaishali Deshmukh**. I also warmly recall **Dr. Vinod Deshmukh** and his wife **Sunanda**, **Dr. Balki**, **Dr. Nasir Kazi**, **Sunanda Chaoji**, **Dr. Saurabh Goel**, **Dr. Pramod Umarji**, **Dr. Suhas Erande**, **Dr. Parimal Lawate**, **Dr. Girish Shah**, **Dr. Amin Khoja**, **Dr. Vedavati Purandare**, and **Dr. Sarika Saklecha**. Each one has added joy and meaning to this journey.

155

They also participated actively in the **BJ Medical College Research Society's Golden Jubilee** and the **Dr. B.B. Dikshit Memorial Oration**, which was organized by the Society and conferred a singular honor upon me as the invited orator. I will always remember that event with deep gratitude and pride.

I am especially thankful to **Dr. Vinod Shah**, my former student, now a respected doctor and social worker, and to his compassionate wife **Meena**, for their long-standing friendship. Their service through the Janata Foundation to the elderly, disabled, and homeless in Maharashtra is deeply inspiring. I am proud to have worked with them on research related to aging.

My special thanks are due to **Dr. Bhushan Patwardhan**, my co-author in past work on integrative health and one of India's leading biomedical scientists, and now the joint author of our forthcoming book "THE OM WAY" for his continued partnership.... I appreciate the support of his dedicated colleague **Dr. Girish Tillu**, an Ayurvedic doctor and teacher at **Savitribai Phule Pune University**, whose shared vision has been uplifting.

I offer my heartfelt thanks to my friends at **Sun City Center**, especially **Balawant and Lata Karlekar**, for their warmth and support during many parts of this journey. They feel like family. I am also grateful to **Mr. Shashi Gude**, his wife **Mrudul**, and their son **Atish** for their kind support and interest in this work. **Mr. Shirish Mulay** and **Dr. Swati Mulay** have helped me in many ways, and **Mr. Samir Padhye**, a devoted follower, has given strong support with deep involvement. I am also thankful to **Mr. Manohar Apte** and **Dr. Sunanda Apte** for their kindness.

I value the friendship and help of **Saroj and Arvind Joshi**, and of **Prof. Rustom Kevala** and **Yasmin Kevala**, who have been close companions. My warm thanks to **Dr. Sadhana Sathe** and **Mr. Sharad Sathe** for our many discussions on the Geeta and Yoga, which brought insight and joy. I also thank the wider **Sun City Center** community for their yoga gatherings and regular get-togethers, which gave me strength and inspiration.

I feel deep respect and gratitude for **Dr. Shyam**, **Kunda**, and **Pushpa Gawande**, who hosted many spiritual sessions. Their lives reflect the ideals of karma yoga. I also thank **Manjiri Vaishampayan**, a gifted singer, and her husband, for sharing beautiful songs and bhajans that inspired us all. I am grateful to my spiritually inclined friends **Vandana and Kirit**, whose presence in our group has been uplifting. They follow the path of **Sri Aurobindo** and are deeply devoted to inner growth. I also thank another wonderful couple, **Mr. George and Sudha Hunziker**, for their principled and inspiring way of life.

My sincere thanks go to **Authors Publishing House** for helping prepare the final manuscript and raising it to a quality suitable for global publication.

Finally, I thank all my readers. I look forward to continuing our journey together as fellow seekers, as we explore how to live with wisdom, courage, and compassion in the face of the challenges of our time. I am truly grateful that you are walking this path with me.

Index

Author Biography

Dr. Gururaj Mutalik is a retired senior physician of international repute. He was born in March 1929 into an orthodox rural family in Karnataka, India. His father was a traditional scholar who excelled in Vedanta, Sanskrit, and the practice of Ayurveda. Dr. Mutalik's father introduced all his children to the study of Sanskrit, Yoga, and Vedanta.

Dr. Mutalik earned his medical degrees and began an illustrious career in academic medicine. He served in a national capacity in India as professor and chair of a department of medicine, dean of a medical school, and Director of Medical Education and Health Services in the state of Maharashtra. Later, he served on three continents as a director at the World Health Organization (WHO) and headed the WHO office at the United Nations headquarters in New York. Throughout his career, Dr. Mutalik championed global health initiatives and contributed to shaping international health policy.

Following his retirement in 1990, he became the Chief Executive Officer of the International Physicians for the Prevention of Nuclear War (IPPNW), an international physicians' organization that received the Nobel Peace Prize in 1985. This organization is dedicated to the promotion of world peace, nuclear disarmament, and human development.

Dr. Mutalik's lifelong passion, however, has been the research, study, and teaching of ancient Indian thought (Sanatana Dharma). He is the author of several books and articles in various fields, including medicine, development, yoga, Ayurveda, and Eastern philosophy.

This book describes his yogic reveries during meditation.

www.ingramcontent.com/pod-product-compliance
Lightning Source LLC
Chambersburg PA
CBHW071952131225
36720CB00001B/1